The Bible Speaks Today

Series editors: J. A. Motyer (OT)
John Stott (NT)
Derek Tidball (Bible Themes)

The Message of Esther

The Message of Esther

God Present But Unseen

DAVID G. FIRTH

IVP Academic
An imprint of InterVarsity Press
Downers Grove, Illinois

InterVarsity Press
P.O. Box 1400, Downers Grove, IL 60515-1426
ivpress.com
email@ivpress.com

InterVarsity Press® is the book-publishing division of InterVarsity Christian Fellowship/USA®, a movement of students and faculty active on campus at hundreds of universities, colleges and schools of nursing in the United States of America, and a member movement of the International Fellowship of Evangelical Students. For information about local and regional activities, visit intervarsity.org.

Cover design: Cindy Kiple
Image: Marilee Whitehouse-Holm/Getty Images

ISBN 978-0-8308-2433-5

Printed in the United States of America ∞

Library of Congress Cataloging-in-Publication Data

Firth, David G.
  The message of Esther: God present but unseen / David G. Firth.
      p. cm.
  Includes bibliographical references.
  ISBN 978-0-8308-2433-5 (pbk.: alk. paper)
  1. Bible. O.T. Esther—Commentaries. I. Title.
  BS1375.53.F57 2010
  222'.907—dc22

                                                                    2010019861

P   22   21   20   19   18   17   16   15   14   13   12   11   10

Y   30   29   28   27   26   25   24   23   22   21

For Pete and Theresa
Discovering God's providence in surprising ways

Contents

BST The Bible Speaks Today

GENERAL PREFACE

THE BIBLE SPEAKS TODAY describes three series of expositions, based on the books of the Old and New Testaments, and on Bible themes that run through the whole of Scripture. Each series is characterized by a threefold ideal:

- to expound the biblical text with accuracy
- to relate it to contemporary life, and
- to be readable.

These books are, therefore, not 'commentaries', for the commentary seeks rather to elucidate the text than to apply it, and tends to be a work rather of reference than of literature. Nor, on the other hand, do they contain the kinds of 'sermons' that attempt to be contemporary and readable without taking Scripture seriously enough. The contributors to *The Bible Speaks Today* series are all united in their convictions that God still speaks through what he has spoken, and that nothing is more necessary for the life, health and growth of Christians than that they should hear what the Spirit is saying to them through his ancient – yet ever modern – Word.

ALEC MOTYER
JOHN STOTT
DEREK TIDBALL
Series editors

Author's preface

My interest in the book of Esther came about in a rather co-incidental way, something appropriate to a book which makes much of coincidence as a means of seeing God at work in our world. In 1990 my wife and I went with the Australian Baptist Missionary Society to Zimbabwe where I was to teach Biblical Studies at the Theological College of Zimbabwe. One of the courses I taught there was an introduction to exegesis, and on the basis of student feedback we decided to give one hour a week to the study of an actual text. The question was which one? Reasoning that I had a ten-week teaching term, so that roughly one chapter a week would be appropriate, and that a narrative was less likely to pose too many major problems, I decided that Esther would suit admirably.

At the time, I had never studied Esther in any detail, though I assumed (rightly as it happened) that none of my students would have done so either, meaning that there would be fewer preconceptions that would impede the actual process of exegesis. In many ways it was therefore a rather pragmatic decision on the basis of a specific set of circumstances, but it was also an inspired one and the weekly sessions on Esther became a highlight of the programme. It also inspired me to study the book further, looking for a while at Esther as the basis for doctoral work, but continuing to study it even when my research took other directions. Since I was frequently moonlighting as a preacher at churches in and around Bulawayo I also took the opportunity to begin exploring exactly how one could communicate what this book had to say for Christians in the midst of increasingly difficult circumstances. When we moved to the Baptist College of Southern Africa in Johannesburg I needed a reading text for the second-year Hebrew students and again drew on Esther since its higher than average number of feminine forms forces students to attend to their parsing. But this made me more aware than before of the subtlety with which the story is told, even though at times it appears to verge more on farce than anything else.

Since then it is a text to which I have turned at a variety of times. I took the opportunity to preach through the whole book with the evening congregation at St Ives Baptist Church in Sydney in 1998, in an extended reading of the story (using the divisions of the text employed here). Several congregation members admitted that they would not read the chapter we were considering until after the service because they were waiting to find out what happened next and did not want to spoil the surprise of the sermon, but then would read it again in light of the exposition. This showed me more clearly than before just how well this story is told and why our own preaching of it must help our congregations be drawn into it if they are to appreciate what it has to say. Most recently, I worked through Esther in a series of talks presented as the 2009 Bible Study at Dronfield Baptist Church – an opportunity to develop and polish my thinking on this generally neglected book.

Telling this story reminds me that my understanding of the text has been formed in community; that this is a story to be told and retold so that believers together can help one another to come to a richer understanding of it. Students and colleagues at various institutions and congregants in a range of churches and settings have all contributed to my understanding of this story and its significance for us today. Studying the Bible is not, finally, something that happens solely as scholars work away in their studies (as vital as this is) but as we work together to hear what God is saying through his Word. Likewise, my family has continued to support and sustain me in my work, and my wife Lynne continues to exercise the gift of encouragement in numerous ways.

Thanks are also due to Alec Motyer, who has been a consistently encouraging editor whilst also challenging me to think through my ideas, and Phil Duce, who has seen the whole process through at IVP with his customary care and diligence. Mentioning all who have helped apart from them probably is impossible, but I would like simply to record my appreciation to Pete and Theresa Phillips who welcomed us like family when we came to England, and also for endless discussions with Pete about aspects of the theory of narrative that have helped me to think through more thoroughly than before how it is that Esther communicates. Dedicating this book to them is a small mark of gratitude.

DAVID G. FIRTH

Chief abbreviations

AJSL	*American Journal of Semitic Languages*
AT	Alpha Text of the book of Esther
ESV	English Standard Version
GNB	Good News Bible
JBL	*Journal of Biblical Literature*
LXX	Septuagint
MT	Masoretic Text
NASB	New American Standard Bible
NIV	New International Version
NRSV	New Revised Standard Version
RSV	Revised Standard Version
ZAW	*Zeitschrift für die Alttestamentliche Wissenschaft*

Bibliography

Anderson, B. W., 'The Book of Esther' in G. W. Buttrick (ed.), *The Interpreter's Bible* vol. 3 (Nashville: Abingdon, 1954), pp. 821–874

——, 'The Place of the Book of Esther in the Christian Bible', *Journal of Religion* 30 (1950), pp. 32–43

Baldwin, J. G., *Esther: An Introduction and Commentary* (Leicester: IVP, 1984)

Bechtel, C. M., *Esther* (Louisville: Westminster John Knox, 2002)

Beckett, M., *Gospel in Esther* (Carlisle: Paternoster, 2002)

Bergey, R. L., 'Post-Exilic Hebrew Linguistic Developments in Esther: A Diachronic Approach', *Journal of the Evangelical Theological Society* 31 (1988), pp. 161–168

Berlin, A. 'The Book of Esther and Ancient Storytelling', *JBL* 120/1 (2001), p. 3–14

——, *Esther: The Traditional Hebrew Text with the New JPS Translation* (Philadelphia: Jewish Publication Society, 2001)

Berg, S. B., *The Book of Esther: Motifs, Themes and Structure* (Missoula: Scholar's Press, 1979)

Breneman, M., *Ezra, Nehemiah, Esther* (Nashville: Broadman & Holman, 1993)

Bush, F., *Ruth/Esther* (Dallas: Word, 1996)

Carson, D. A., *Divine Sovereignty and Human Responsibility: Biblical Perspectives in Tension* (London: Marshall, Morgan & Scott, 1981)

Carruthers, J., *Esther through the Ages* (Oxford: Blackwell, 2008)

Clines, D. J. A., *Ezra, Nehemiah, Esther* (Grand Rapids: Eerdmans, 1984)

——, *The Esther Scroll: The Story of the Story* (Sheffield: JSOT Press, 1984)

——, 'The Quest for the Historical Mordecai', in *Vetus Testamentum* 41 (1991), pp. 129–136

Crawford, S. W., 'Esther', in L. E. Keck (ed.), *The New Interpreter's Bible*, vol. 3 (Nashville: Abingdon, 1999), pp. 853–942

Day, L. M., *Esther* (Nashville: Abingdon, 2005)

Dickson, C. R., *The Role And Portrayal Of The King In The Esther Narrative: A Narratological-Synchronic reading of the Masoretic text of the Esther Narrative* (Unpublished PhD Thesis, University of Pretoria, 1999)

Dommershausen, W., *Die Estherrolle: Stil und Ziel einer alttestamentlichen Schrift* (Stuttgart: Verlag Katholisches Bibelwerk, 1968)

Dorothy, C. V., *The Books of Esther: Structure, Genre and Textual Integrity* (Sheffield: Sheffield Academic Press, 1997)

Firth, D. G., 'The Book of Esther: A Neglected Paradigm for Dealing with the State', *Old Testament Essays* 10 (1997), pp. 18–26

———, 'The Third Quest for the Historical Mordecai and the Genre of the Book of Esther', *Old Testament Essays* 16 (2003), pp. 233–243

Fox, M. V., *The Redaction of the Books of Esther: On Reading Composite Texts* (Atlanta: Scholar's Press, 1991)

———, *Character and Ideology in the Book of Esther* (2nd ed., Grand Rapids: Eerdmans, 2001)

Goldman, S., 'Narrative and Ethical Ironies in Esther', *Journal for Study of the Old Testament* 47 (1990), pp. 15–31

Gordis, R., 'Studies in the Esther Narrative', *Journal of Biblical Literature* 95 (1976), pp. 43–58

———, 'Religion, Wisdom and History in the Book of Esther – a New Solution to an Ancient Crux', *Journal of Biblical Literature* 100 (1981), pp. 359–388

Haupt, P., 'Critical Notes on Esther', *AJSL* 24 (1907–8), pp. 97–186

Huey, F. B.,'Esther', in F. E. Gaebelein (ed.), *The Expositor's Bible Commentary*, vol. 4 (Grand Rapids: Zondervan, 1988), pp. 775–839

Humphreys, W. L., 'A Life-Style for the Diaspora: A Study of the Tales of Esther and Daniel', *Journal of Biblical Literature* 92 (1975), pp. 211–223

Jobes, K. H., *Esther: The NIV Application Commentary* (Grand Rapids: Zondervan, 1999)

Klaasen, M. J., 'Persian/Jew/Jew/Persian: Levels of Irony in the Scroll of Esther', *Direction* 25 (1996), pp. 21–28

Laniak, T. S., 'Esther', in L. C. Allen and T. S. Laniak, *Ezra, Nehemiah, Esther* (Peabody: Hendrickson, 2003), pp. 169–270

Levenson, J. D., *Esther: A Commentary* (London: SCM Press, 1997)

Loader, J. A., 'Esther as a Novel with Various Levels of Meaning', *ZAW* 90, pp. 417–421

McConville, J. G., *Ezra, Nehemiah, Esther* (Edinburgh: St Andrew's Press, 1985)

Moore, C. A., *Esther* (Garden City: Doubleday, 1971)

——, 'Archaeology and the Book of Esther', *Biblical Archaeology* 38 (1975), pp. 62–79

Morris, A. E., 'The Purpose of the Book of Esther', *Expository Times* 42 (1930–31), pp. 124–128

Murphy, G. L., 'Providence and Passion in Esther', *Currents in Theology and Mission* 29 (2002), pp. 122–127

Peels, E., *Shadow Sides: God in the Old Testament* (Carlisle: Paternoster, 2003)

Paton, L. B., *A Critical and Exegetical Commentary on the Book of Esther* (Edinburgh: T & T Clark, 1908)

Reid, D., *Esther: An Introduction and Commentary* (Nottingham: IVP, 2008)

Roberts, M. D., *Ezra, Nehemiah, Esther* (Dallas: Word, 1993)

Rodriguez, A. M., *Esther: A Theological Approach* (Berrien Springs: Andrews University Press, 1995)

Talmon, S., ' "Wisdom" in the Book of Esther', *Vetus Testamentum* 13 (1963), pp. 419–455

Ungnad, A., 'Keilinschriftliche Beiträge zum Buch Esra und Esther', *ZAW* 58 (1940), pp. 240–244

Webb, B. G., *Five Festal Garments: Christian Reflections on the Song of Songs, Ruth, Lamentations, Ecclesiastes and Esther* (Leicester: Apollos, 2000)

Weiland, F. S., 'Historicity, Genre and Narrative Design in the Book of Esther', *Bibliotheca Sacra* 159 (2002), pp. 151–165

——, 'Literary Clues to God's Providence in the Book of Esther', *Bibliotheca Sacra* 160 (2003), pp. 34–47

——, 'Literary Conventions in the Book of Esther', *Bibliotheca Sacra* 159 (2002), pp. 425–435

——, 'Plot Structure in the Book of Esther', *Bibliotheca Sacra* 159 (2002), pp. 277–287

Wiebe, J. M., 'Will Relief and Deliverance Arise for the Jews from Another Place?' *Catholic Biblical Quarterly* 53 (1991), pp. 409–415

Yamauchi, E. M., 'The Archaeologial Background of Esther', *Bibliotheca Sacra* 137 (1980), pp. 99–117

Introduction

By any assessment, Esther is a rather strange book to find in the Bible. Not only is it, along with Daniel, the only book of the Bible to be set entirely outside of the Promised Land, it also shows no interest in that land, unlike Daniel who made it the point of orientation for his prayer.[1] More than that, Esther is the only book in the Bible which definitely does not mention God,[2] though this has not stopped people trying to find references to God hidden in acrostics in the text. For example, the successive words in the phrase, 'let the king and Haman come today',[3] in Hebrew start with the letters that make up the name commonly written as Yahweh, God's covenant name in the Old Testament. Somewhat more ingeniously, the last letter of each word in the phrase 'all this is worth nothing to me'[4] also contain the letters of the divine name, though this time we are required to read the words backwards to find it. As impressive as such things might seem, it is unlikely that these are anything more than accidents of composition. Since the letters required to make the name Yahweh are actually very common we would need to have evidence that the phenomenon is significantly more common in the book of Esther than it is to believe that there is anything intentional in it, quite apart from the question of why we would be expected to observe an acrostic of the last letter of each word that we have to read backwards even to notice that it is there. In fact, as we shall see, the book of Esther not only fails to mention God at all, but it also seems to go out of its way to avoid any obviously religious language, so that attempts to hide God within the language of the text would actually be counter to its purposes. None of this should be taken as meaning that the

[1] Dan. 6:10.
[2] The Song of Songs may or may not mention God, depending on how we translate 8:6.
[3] 5:4.
[4] 5:13.

19

book has no theological intention. On the contrary it has a developed theology, but it is a theology which operates precisely because it does not mention God directly. It is this paradox which both makes Esther such a strange book within the Bible and yet at the same time one which is of great importance for those of us living in post-Christendom, where we need to live out our faith in a world where we often cannot name God directly. Thus, what might seem on the surface to be a rather odd book is actually one that invites us to reflect on what it is to know God within this world – a world where the miraculous is rare and yet in which the faithful continue to experience the reality of God's presence.

1. Which Esther?

Before considering other matters we have to start with one basic but perhaps unusual question. Which book of Esther should we read? The importance of this emerges from the fact that three different versions of the book have come down to us, each with its own emphases[5] and character.[6] Our first decision must therefore be to determine which of these stories we need to interpret.

The best-known version of Esther, and the one represented in most editions of the Bible today, is that found in the Hebrew text[7] which underlies the Protestant Old Testament. This version of the story does not mention God, and seems to go out of its way to avoid mention of religious themes and practices other than fasting.[8] The difficulty of a text which does not mention God is addressed by the next-best-known version of Esther. This is a Greek version which includes some extra passages known as Additions A–F.[9] These additions are included in printed additions of the Apocrypha as a separate work known as 'The Additions to Esther', although no manuscript exists which does not have them included within this version of the book. These additions include extensive religious

---

[5] One could add to these three the variations found in the Targum and Josephus, but these are retellings, and so excluded from this discussion. See C. V. Dorothy, *The Books of Esther: Structure, Genre and Textual Integrity* (Sheffield: Sheffield Academic Press, 1997), pp. 13–16.

[6] The most complete discussion of the relationship of these versions of the story is M. V. Fox, *The Redaction of the Books of Esther* (Atlanta: Scholar's Press, 1991), though it is helpful first to read D. J. A. Clines, *The Esther Scroll: The Story of the Story* (Sheffield: JSOT Press, 1984). Fox provides a helpful summary of his views in, *idem*, *Character and Ideology in the Books of Esther*, 2nd ed. (Grand Rapids: Eerdmans, 2001), pp. 254–273.

[7] Known as the Masoretic Text (MT).

[8] 4:1–3.

[9] Known as the Septuagint (or LXX).

material so that the book now commences with Mordecai's dream (Addition A) in which God reveals to him what is about to happen, as well as prayers and the like. But once we remove the additions we discover that this is more or less a translation of the story as it appears in the Hebrew text. Since the additions are clearly secondary and distract us from the central narrative we can discount them beyond noting that they show an early concern with the book's apparent lack of reference to God.

The third form of the Esther story that has come down to us is in an alternative Greek text.[10] This appears to be a translation of a somewhat different Hebrew original. This form of the story is much less accessible to most readers today, but Clines has helpfully produced both the Greek text and an English translation.[11] The manuscripts we have of this version also include Additions A–F, but they are clearly not an original part of it. With these removed we are left with a story that is recognisably that of Esther but which has significant variations, possibly ending with Mordecai's elevation at the end of chapter 8, meaning there is no link with Purim. Like the Hebrew form of Esther it probably does not mention God though it does mention prayer.[12] For a variety of reasons, this is probably the earliest version of the story of Esther, but that the story existed in an earlier form does not make it more important for us. That slightly variant forms of the story existed is not in itself surprising as stories can be passed on for a variety of reasons – we only need to consider the way we often tell stories from our own experience to illustrate different issues to recognise this. But the Hebrew form of Esther was ultimately recognised as the canonical form, because its telling of the story was most appropriate. As such, although we will occasionally note variants from the other forms of the story, this exposition focuses on the book of Esther as it occurs in printed editions of the Bible, but without reference to the Additions.

2. Genre and purpose

Knowing that Esther might have been told in other ways helps us recognise some of the book's key emphases, but it does not resolve the question of exactly what sort of literature this is. Asking a question like this means we are enquiring about the book's genre, which we can define as that set of characteristics that define the way in which it is meant to be read and interpreted. At a most basic level, we recognise that we interpret prose and poetry differently from

[10] Known as the Alpha Text (AT).
[11] Clines, *The Esther Scroll*, pp. 215–248.
[12] AT 5:11, which is roughly equivalent to MT 4:16.

one another, but we also appreciate that we interpret different forms of prose differently too. Hence, we read a work of history differently from a work of fiction, but we don't read all works of history or fiction in the same way. We would read a James Bond novel differently from Aesop's fables, and both are different from Jesus' parables. Now, the biblical writers did not generally work with the same sets of genres as we do today because genres vary across languages and cultures. But the biblical authors still chose the genres they did because they enabled them to communicate their message. Our task is to understand the genre employed so we can understand the message the biblical writers wanted to communicate.

At the risk of over-simplifying a complex debate,[13] scholars have generally reached two basic views on the book's genre, though a mediating position has emerged. The classical view was that Esther was a historical work, reflecting a deliverance of the Jews in Persia. But this view was radically challenged by Paton.[14] Although not the first to do so, he systematically attacked it, highlighting a number of alleged historical inconsistencies (such as the fact that we know of no Jewish queen in Persia from other sources) and concluding that because of these factors Esther had to be a work of fiction. This has become the dominant critical view of the book. Yet it is fundamentally flawed because it assumes that ancient writers should follow our historical conventions rather than those of their time. This does not itself disprove Paton's conclusion, merely that the argument itself is flawed, but it does mean that we need to approach the whole issue more carefully.

The basic alternative is to regard Esther as an historical work. It is certainly possible to link the events described in the book with other historical sources.[15] This approach takes seriously the presence of certain features within the book which suggest historical intent, such as the reference to Mordecai in the Chronicles of Media and Persia,[16] though it would help if we actually had a copy of this chronicle! But although we can draw on these sources, we still need to concede Clines' point that archaeological information is only relevant if we can establish from the text that the book was written

[13] For a more detailed overview, see D. G. Firth, 'The Third Quest for the Historical Mordecai and the Genre of the Book of Esther', *Old Testament Essays* 16 (2003), pp. 233–243.

[14] L. B. Paton, *A Critical and Exegetical Commentary on the Book of Esther* (Edinburgh: T & T Clark, 1908), pp. 64–77.

[15] For a possible identification of Mordecai, see Arthur Ungnad, 'Keilinschriftliche Beiträge zum Buch Esra und Esther', *ZAW* 58 (1940), pp. 240–244. Cf. R. Gordis, 'Religion, Wisdom and History in the Book of Esther – A New Solution to an Old Crux', *JBL* 100 (1981), p. 375.

[16] 10:2.

with an historical intent.[17] In a sense, therefore, both those who have argued for the book's historicity and those who have argued it is a work of fiction have made the same generic error of looking for external factors to determine the book's genre rather than working from the hints provided by the text itself.

Hence, consideration of this issue must start with the text, though in doing so we must admit that we do not have definitions of genre that were available to ancient readers of the Hebrew Bible. In terms of history we can note times where the text refers to points that can be verified – thus the opening reference to Ahasuerus[18] seems to indicate that this is not a discussion of an abstracted figure but rather someone whose nature and identity can be traced. Likewise, the closing reference to Mordecai[19] also suggests that he can be recognised from historical sources available to the author and (presumably) at least some of the original readers. Yet this has not convinced everyone. For example, Berlin argues that these references should not be taken as historical, drawing an analogy to Hans Christian Andersen's story, 'The Princess and the Pea.'[20] That story refers to a pea which could still be seen in a museum because of its role in identifying a true princess, although it is clear that this is simply part of the conceit Andersen adopts. According to Berlin, the apparent reference to historical sources in Esther can be accounted for in the same way. But this argument only holds if we have evidence that ancient writers employed such a technique within fiction, and the absence of evidence for this suggests that ancient readers would struggle to recognise it here. As such, we should conclude that the book is intended to be read as having a basic level of historical reference,[21] though in noting this we still have to assess the qualities of that intent, especially since Esther also shows advanced skills in storytelling, particularly highlighting apparent coincidences.

Thus, the book's internal hints suggest the need for a mediating position, one that considers both its historical references and storytelling. This option appears to have first been suggested by Moore[22] who argued that there was nothing in Esther that could not have happened, though neither was there any significant evidence that it

---

[17] D. J. A. Clines, 'The Quest for the Historical Mordecai', *Vetus Testamentum*, 1991, p. 136.

[18] 1:1.

[19] 10:2.

[20] A. Berlin, 'The Book of Esther and Ancient Storytelling', *JBL* 120/1 (2001), p. 7.

[21] Similarly, T. S. Laniak, 'Esther', in Leslie C. Allen and Timothy S. Laniak, *Ezra, Nehemiah, Esther* (Peabody: Hendrickson, 2003), p. 178.

[22] C. A. Moore, 'Archaeology and the Book of Esther', *BA* 38 (1975), pp. 62–79.

did. Moore still tended to the view that there was strong evidence against the book's historicity at certain points, but believed there might be an historical kernel. A more helpful position is developed by Jobes, who argues that it is inappropriate to set narrative skill against historicity and thus tending to support the book's historical foundation while still emphasising its narrative skill.[23] We will note some of the historical problems when considering the main characters below, but in general a mediating position seems sound as it considers both the historical references within the text, which suggest some historical foundation, and also the evident use of the storyteller's art, a point which proponents for the fictional view have emphasised. We thus confront the problem that our own world lacks a functioning generic model with which to read the book of Esther, though perhaps 'dramatized history' comes closest.

This highlights the important point that, just because one concludes that a text has an historical reference, this does not mean we have discerned its purpose, because history is almost always someone preaching from the past to their contemporaries. In considering Esther we must therefore note the importance of 9:20 – 10:3 and its emphasis on not only celebrating Purim, but also doing so in a way that is both celebratory and reflective, an emphasis which derives from letters sent by both Mordecai and Esther. These verses are clearly an addition to the story, but they are there to offer some guidance on how to read the story, though it is safe to observe that Esther cannot fully account for Purim and neither can Purim fully account for Esther.[24] The book of Esther offers a historical context for the celebration of Purim; but because Purim itself plays such a minor role within the narrative, we need to look more broadly and recognise that it can have multiple purposes.

This in turn points us to the great skill with which the story is told. The narrative's literary artistry has been much praised, and it is certainly true that the book of Esther represents a high point in the art of storytelling within the Old Testament. Esther is meant to be enjoyed. In my own experience, a careful reading of 6:1–13 often has the congregation laughing at all the right points, meaning that they intuitively 'get' the point of that part of the story although there remains much to be said. But the crucial point to make is that although the book of Esther refers to historical events, it does so in a way that intends to entertain. It is not enough to know that there

[23] K. H. Jobes, *Esther: The NIV Application Commentary* (Grand Rapids: Zondervan, 1999), pp. 30–32.

[24] S. B. Berg, *The Book of Esther: Motifs, Themes and Structure* (Missoula: Scholar's Press, 1979), p. 4.

was a time of deliverance in Persia. Rather, we learn and remember this most effectively because we are entertained by it.

In considering the book's purpose, it is worth noting that Esther is set entirely outside of Israel, and never refers to it apart from an incidental occurrence when mentioning the exile in 2:6. A particularly important question – one that the exile particularly triggered – was whether to remain faithful within a world where Jews were a minority and how this was possible. This may be one reason why the book of Esther does not mention God directly. The assumed religious dialogue of the Diaspora was not one where it could be assumed that reference to God automatically meant Israel's God, Yahweh. As well as modelling both the possibilities and limits of engagement with the dominant culture, Esther also points to God's presence amongst his people in a way that they would recognise, but without misleading others. God's presence is veiled, though when we recognise this we need to appreciate that peering through the veil still leaves us with some ambiguity.[25] This is because, although the story is told in a way that evokes other parts of the Old Testament, the narrator never tells us exactly what God has done. That God is active among his people even in the Diaspora is essential to the book, and we are meant to recognise this, but how much of God's activity depends upon the faithfulness of his people and how much is God's direct involvement is a question that is raised but never answered directly. But it is clear that his people can live in the Diaspora and remain faithful to God who also remains faithful to them. Within post-Christendom, a period where it can no longer be assumed that the dominant religious discourse is that of Christianity, this models an important pattern for us to consider in our telling of how God in Christ is at work in, among, and through his people.

3. Main characters

Since the main historical questions associated with Esther and its literary techniques come together in our understanding of the principal characters within the book, it is worthwhile to consider them at this point. It should be noted that beyond the four main characters – Ahasuerus, Mordecai, Esther and Haman – Esther has a wide range of other figures who contribute to the narrative. This is somewhat unusual in that, while the Old Testament is frequently content to leave minor characters (and sometimes even important ones) anonymous, Esther delights in naming most of them for us,

---

[25] See M. V. Fox, *Character and Ideology in the Book of Esther*, pp. 246–247.

[handwritten margin note: People who have been spread or have been dispersed from their homeland]

even going to the level of identifying figures like the seven eunuchs who were sent to summon Vashti to the king's party.[26] Not every character is named – for example, the attendants who suggested to Ahasuerus that he should gather all the beautiful virgins in the Empire to find a replacement for Vashti[27] – but on the whole the preference is to name characters where possible. Against this, we should note that we are usually given little more than a name and the information needed to place a character in relation to others, a pattern consistent with the book's general reticence at providing more information than what the principal characters can see. Naming gives us a sense of verisimilitude, though in fact most of the Persian names appear to be corrupted, suggesting a faint mocking of Persian pretensions even as we are told about them. Indeed, all the Persian characters appear somewhat cartoon-like, and the pattern of naming may point to this. This pattern also shows the importance of Esther and Mordecai more clearly.

a. Ahasuerus

The first character to whom we are introduced is the Persian king Ahasuerus. His reign provides the context in which we are to set the story[28] while his power and prestige are immediately indicated by the extended celebrations he organises in 1:1–9. That much is clear, but can we identify this king? LXX calls him Artaxerxes, though most English versions present the name as Xerxes, identifying him with a king whose reign is known to us from Herodotus. Although it may not seem terribly obvious in English, both Ahasuerus and Xerxes are probably derived from the Persian name *xšayāršā*, with the differences stemming from the processes by which one name arrived in English via Hebrew and the other through Greek. As such, it seems that the LXX's rendering of the name as Artaxerxes (Xerxes' son) represents a misplaced exegetical guess rather than something that should guide our reading. Although the book of Esther and Herodotus do not characterise the king in exactly the same way (Esther does not record the evidence for cruelty we find in Herodotus), there is enough in common for us to believe they are discussing the same king.

If we are right in identifying Ahasuerus with Xerxes, then we have a satisfactory background for reading the book. Xerxes reigned from 485–465 BC, and is perhaps best known for his unsuccessful attempts at taking control of Greece. Xerxes inherited the kingdom

[26] 1:10.
[27] 2:2.
[28] 1:1–2.

from Darius I, but took over in a time of unrest, with separate revolts in both 485 and 484. The book opens with his celebrations in the third year of his reign,[29] and its firm establishment would provide a context for this since such displays both rewarded the faithful and warned others of the danger of revolt. This was also when he made his plans to attack Greece, though this ended badly with his defeat at Salamis in 480. He then returned home in the seventh year of his reign seeking comfort from his harem.[30] This is also the year when Esther came to prominence,[31] suggesting that the narrator intends us to read the story against this background. There are still problems with this identification, but as these are mainly to do with the identity of his wife, we shall note those when considering Esther.

As helpful as this background is, it tells us comparatively little about how the book of Esther wants us to understand Ahasuerus. He is clearly a powerful king, but he is also a buffoon who is driven by the combination of wine and a desire for honour. He shares this combination with Haman, but an important distinction between them is that Ahasuerus is a consistently unknowing figure. His great feasts in 1:1–9 are intended to proclaim his power and authority, but all this is undermined when his then queen Vashti refused to attend the party. Ahasuerus' problem, fuelled by alcohol, was that he had no idea how to handle this and needed the assistance of his state advisors to deal with what is effectively a family difficulty. Likewise, when he had deposed Vashti he needed his attendants' advice to concoct a scheme for finding a replacement.[32] More culpably, he agreed to issue a decree for the destruction of all the Jews without ever bothering to find out who was to be destroyed.[33] Although Dickson has shown that the king is not quite as dim as some have suggested,[34] it is perhaps better to say that his more insightful moments are examples of native cunning than anything else. Thus, he finally condemns Haman for a crime he has not committed[35] whilst subsequently claiming to have condemned him for his plot against the Jews.[36] What is vital to the narrative is that this is a malleable king, someone controlled by the interests of those

---

[29] 1:3.
[30] Herodotus, 9.180.
[31] 2:16.
[32] 2:1–4.
[33] 3:8–11.
[34] Charles R. Dickson, *The Role and Portrayal of the King in the Esther Narrative: A Narratological – Synchronic Reading of the Masoretic Text of the Esther Narrative* (unpublished PhD thesis, University of Pretoria, 1999).
[35] 7:8.
[36] 8:7.

around him even though he believes himself to be the great and powerful king. In effect, he becomes a figure through which the book of Esther mocks Persian pretensions, hinting that there is a better alternative, though leaving it to readers to work out what that alternative is.

b. Mordecai

Whereas it is possible to identify Ahasuerus, connecting Mordecai with any known Persian figures is probably an impossible task. As noted above, some have attempted to link him with a *Marduka* mentioned in a text from the period, but it is probably better to leave this as evidence that he bore a name known from the time than to formalise the connection simply because we lack the necessary evidence. Of course, if the Chronicles of Media and Persia[37] were to be unearthed then we could expect reference to him, but even allowing for his ultimate rank within the Persian Empire, a lack of reference to him in contemporary sources outside of Esther is no surprise. As such, our main concern here can be with the way he is presented within the book.

A key question which has never been resolved fully is whether Mordecai or Esther is the book's human hero. Given that they operate as a team it is probable that this is incapable of resolution, though there are clearly points where Mordecai is the leading figure. Mordecai's importance is evident from his introduction,[38] which places him in the context of Israel's wider history. He is introduced as a Jew (here an ethnic term since he is from the tribe of Benjamin) whose importance can be seen from his genealogy. This genealogy links him with Saul[39] since they share the names of several ancestors, though of course they are separated by several centuries. The importance of this parallel is the way the allusion to Saul then becomes an important element for the rest of the book, especially in Mordecai's conflict with Haman. Mordecai is also defined in terms of the exile, though it is more likely that his ancestor Kish was the one exiled since Mordecai would otherwise be too old. Equally important in his introduction is the fact that he cares for his cousin Esther, care that contrasts sharply with the conspicuous consumption of the Persians.

Although Mordecai cared for Esther there were clearly limits he would not transgress in working out what it means to be faithful. The most important of these was his refusal to bow down to

---

[37] 10:2.
[38] 2:5–7.
[39] 1 Sam. 9:1–2.

Haman, in spite of the king's order. Mordecai had already demonstrated his general loyalty to the king in revealing a plot to kill him,[40] so he was not opposed in principal to obeying the king. Rather, Mordecai had to balance the demands of living as a faithful Jew with the challenges of being a minority within the Empire. What he could not know was that his decision not to bow down to Haman, along with the revelation that he was Jewish, would trigger a pogrom against all Jews throughout the Empire. The book is careful never to blame Mordecai for this, not only because it is improper to blame victims for what others do, but also because this was triggered by Mordecai's faithfulness. His faithfulness to his people is then shown as he persuaded Esther to act,[41] before fading from the story until his introduction to the king[42] (other than when Haman had to honour him).[43] That he distinguished between Haman's criminal intent and the importance of peace within the Empire is then shown in the careful way he worked within Persian law to overcome Haman's decree,[44] and also to promote Jewish welfare within the empire.[45] Mordecai is thus an important political figure, showing this was possible, but he was also a religious one through his part in introducing Purim's celebration.[46] Mordecai thus demonstrates that one can be a faithful believer and a trustworthy citizen, though matters of faith come first.

c. Esther

Esther is first introduced to us through her relationship with her cousin and guardian Mordecai.[47] She also had a Hebrew name, Hadassah, though her Persian name is used through the rest of the book, and her own genealogy is provided when she went to the king.[48] As we first see her, Esther has two primary characteristics – her beauty and her loyalty to Mordecai. Both of these are important. Her beauty led to her being brought into the harem, and her loyalty meant she did not disclose her ethnicity, enabling her to work for the Jews' deliverance. More than any other, Esther develops and grows within the narrative. Where she is initially dependent on Mordecai, once she has accepted that she must work for her people's

[40] 2:21–23.
[41] 4:1–16.
[42] 8:1–2.
[43] 6:11–13.
[44] 8:9–14.
[45] 10:1–3.
[46] 9:20–28.
[47] 2:7.
[48] 2:15.

deliverance she is then the one who begins to issue orders as she takes on her responsibilities, first directing Mordecai[49] and ultimately all the Jews.[50] Moreover, where chapter 2 emphasised her beauty, the central narrative in chapters 5 – 7, in which Esther takes the lead, stresses her wisdom. The care with which she establishes the possibility of deliverance for the Jews here makes her the personification of wisdom, though it is also clear that wisdom alone would not have sufficed. Nevertheless, she is like Mordecai in that she demonstrates the possibility of working with the Empire as the member of an ethnic and religious minority, with the links to the wisdom literature demonstrating the importance of doing so in terms of Israel's traditions. At the same time, this means balancing conflicting demands, so that she clearly does not eat kosher food, and of course must become a member of a pagan king's harem. Esther's position forces her to make compromises that Mordecai does not, suggesting that within a foreign context there is an order of priorities that were needed if one were to be faithful. Nevertheless, it is her commitment to her people, and thus her faith, that finally drives her,[51] and in this she too models what it means to live as one of God's people as a minority within another context.

But can we identify Esther with any known historical figures? The only wife of Ahasuerus otherwise known to us is called Amestris,[52] not Esther or Vashti. Although the possibility that Esther is a variant for Amestris is sometimes raised,[53] it is improbable. Quite apart from the cruelty which Herodotus attributes to Amestris, she was also the mother of Ahasuerus' son Artaxerxes, whose birth was probably a year before Esther's accession. Associating Vashti with Amestris is also difficult. However, we know that Ahasuerus' relationship with Amestris was very poor and that for much of his reign she was a marginal figure. After his defeat by the Greeks he sought comfort in his harem, which must have existed already. If so, then the title 'queen' may be used loosely within the book to refer to the favoured figure within the harem, the one who functioned much as the queen would even if the position was not formally held. That Esther receives the 'royal crown'[54] is no impediment to this reading because she would still have been

---

[49] 4:17.

[50] 9:29–32.

[51] 4:15–16.

[52] Herodotus, 9.112.

[53] E.g., V. P. Hamilton, *Handbook on the Historical Books* (Grand Rapids: Baker Academic, 2001), p. 533.

[54] 2:17.

acknowledged in some way. This means we cannot identify Esther from sources outside the book, but understanding her as the senior member of the harem is also a plausible way of placing her within the structure of the Persian Empire.

d. Haman

The last of the central characters introduced is Haman. While the others are introduced in a way that tells us something of their character, Haman's introduction is deliberately sudden and unexpected.[55] At the point where we expect Mordecai to be honoured, Haman suddenly comes to prominence. Nevertheless, introducing him as an 'Agagite' creates an immediate link to 1 Samuel 15, where Saul was directed to devote the Amalekites to destruction, but (along with the best livestock) spared their king Agag. His family associations thus place him among a people that had been Israel's enemies since the journey to Sinai, so although his decision to destroy all the Jews, when he realised Mordecai was not honouring him, is shocking it is not surprising. That Haman is driven by honour will also be the cause of his downfall. Having enjoyed his first dinner with the king and queen,[56] he had returned home exulting – except when he again noticed Mordecai failing to honour him, leading ultimately to his wife advising him that the best way to enjoy dinner with them the next day was to impale Mordecai on a stake at their house. Haman duly spent the night erecting this and then arrived at the palace early to arrange Mordecai's execution. But the narrator breaks with the pattern of the rest of the book to show Haman's own drive for honour, when he is caught off guard by the king's sudden question about how to grant honours,[57] a drive which derailed him from his intent, and saw him honour Mordecai instead. In place of honour, he received shame, and in the ensuing events lost control of what was happening and was ultimately condemned by Ahasuerus for attempting to assault Esther.

Haman embodies all that was dangerous for the Diaspora Jews. He came from a people who were long opposed to them and was prepared to make his own drive for honour the factor which he placed before all others. The book of Esther at several points seems to allude to anti-Jewish sentiment, but Haman is its ultimate expression. Haman also stands in contrast to Esther. Where Esther functions as a representative wise woman, Haman evokes descriptions of the fool in Israel's wisdom traditions. Like the king, he is a

[55] 3:1.
[56] 5:4–8.
[57] 6:6.

cartoon figure who does nothing by half measures, but in the end he reveals himself as both an enemy of God's people and a fool, though these categories are not separate from one another. Unsurprisingly, we cannot connect Haman with any known figures from other sources.

e. The Jews

Somewhat unusually, the book of Esther refers consistently to 'the Jews'. More typically, the Old Testament speaks of the people of God as 'Israel' whereas in the New Testament 'the Jews' are those whose religious faith was Judaism, though sometimes the term means only those who were their political or religious leaders. Yet the book of Esther's preferred term is 'the Jews' and I have used it throughout this exposition. Esther's language is in fact indicative of an important linguistic change that is evident in the century after the exile, and may even have reached back into the exile itself. We see evidence of this change in several passages in Ezra[58] and Nehemiah.[59] The term rendered 'Jew' in Esther is often an ethnic marker,[60] but the reference in 8:17, where 'many ... declared themselves Jews' seems to be considerably more than this, possibly indicating a change in religious faith. Similarly, although Mordecai is a Benjaminite, he is also 'the Jew'. His family had been exiled from Jerusalem[61] and so had an important geographical association with Judah, but that he is a 'Jew' must here mean more than that he had an association with Judah. The label 'Jew' in the book of Esther is thus close to its point of emergence and fuses religious and ethnic connotations, frequently moving between them.

Because words develop and change their meaning means we must also be careful not to project other senses of the term onto the book. For evidence of this we need only note the fact that the term came to have a much more specific meaning by the time of the New Testament even if we can (to some extent) trace it on from Esther. The Jews of the book of Esther are not those who opposed Jesus in the Gospels. Equally, we must guard against assuming an automatic correlation between the Jews of Esther and contemporary Judaism, just as we must also guard against the easy assumption that something which uses the label 'Christian' is representative of the gospel. Judaism as we now know it was beginning to emerge at the time of

---

[58] Ezra 4:12, 23; 5:1, 5; 6:7–8, 14.
[59] Neh. 4:1–2.
[60] This also represents the fact that the region around Jerusalem was known by the Persians as Yehud, which is based on the same word.
[61] 2:5.

the events of this book, and the Jews of Esther are in part among its forebears, but if the gospel also emerges out of the Old Testament then they are also among the forebears of the church. They are part of the great story of the people of God, and their deliverance is an important pointer to the greater deliverance that was to come.

4. Reading Esther in light of the canon

Esther is thus a more unusual book than we might initially realise. It tells a story that could be told in various ways, so the form in which we have it is only one possibility for it. More than anything else, therefore, this encourages us to consider exactly how it tells this story because although it makes historical reference, its focus on storytelling requires us to consider this when interpreting it. This focus causes us to look at both the characters and the plot, though the deliberate decision not to tell us what motivates the characters invites us to explore their motives through the story's telling. This also begins to show us how we are to understand Esther as a theological text. Unlike most of the Old Testament's narrative texts which make clear where Yahweh is involved, Esther almost always leaves us only with the information available to the characters within the narrative. None of them know exactly what God is doing while things are happening. Appreciation of God's involvement is something that is only appreciated with hindsight, though this does not stop us from reflecting on our own experiences to consider this. The book of Esther takes this a step further, inviting us to reflect on this story in light of what we know about God from elsewhere in the canon. God may be veiled, and peering behind the veil may not remove the ambiguity inherent in understanding God, but it is something we are called to do.

More than any other text in the Old Testament, Esther asks us to read it in light of the canon of Scripture. One could contend that we look for God in Esther only because its place within the Old Testament compels us to read it religiously, seeking theological themes because the nature of the canon leads us to look for what is not otherwise there. But this is a cynical view of the canon, and even in considering the book's main characters it has been impossible to avoid reference to other parts of the Old Testament. Thus, the introductions to both Mordecai and Haman direct us to 1 Samuel, and then to Exodus 17 to understand the conflict between Israel and Amalek. Esther and Haman respectively embody the wise and the fool from Israel's wisdom traditions, though without thereby becoming ciphers for these figures. They remain responsible individuals, yet their stories are told so that those who know the wisdom traditions cannot help but note the connections. Once we realise that so much of the story is told in a way that alludes to other passages in the Old Testament we begin to realise that our reading of Esther is meant to be shaped by what we know from these other passages and these allusions are consistently theological in their emphases.

To take only one example, the conflict between Haman and Mordecai reaches back to Saul's failure to destroy the Amalekite king Agag in 1 Samuel 15, but this in turn takes us back to Yahweh's declared intent to blot out Amalek in Exodus 17:14. Read in light of these texts we understand why Haman's plot, for all the monstrous power he summons, cannot succeed. Deliverance must come because it is Yahweh's will that Israel overcome Amalek. One could imagine that this would happen without human involvement – Yahweh has promised and in his sovereignty it will simply come to pass. But by simultaneously evoking the wisdom traditions Esther also insists on the importance of the faithfulness of God's people. This is not just a matter of 'taking God for granted',[62] but rather insisting that there is something important in bringing our own lives into the purposes of God. How we do this thus requires us to reflect on both the wisdom tradition and the covenant history of Israel, so that these two elements mutually inform one another. Oddly enough, within the field of Old Testament theology the question of how wisdom and covenant relate remains unsolved and it is perhaps no coincidence that Esther likewise plays a minimal role in most works in this field. But this is to take only a limited sampling of how Esther points us to other texts in the Old Testament so our understanding of them and Esther is enriched by the conversation. Again, to mention only a few examples, Esther makes numerous references to the Joseph story, the exodus traditions, Joshua, Judges and the books of Samuel, as well as allusions to various texts from the prophets. We are not seeking God in a text where he is absent. Rather, we are having our understanding of God enriched by the conversation that is generated. Yet for all this, the skill of the story-telling means that even readers who do not have the canonical background can appreciate God's presence in the story through the coincidences it employs, so even those with only a minimal awareness of the rest of Scripture can appreciate the theological themes developed here.

Christians looking for further insights from the New Testament will be disappointed to note that apart from a few slight allusions

---

[62] D. J. A. Clines, *Ezra, Nehemiah, Esther* (Grand Rapids: Eerdmans, 1984), p. 271. To be fair to Clines, he means this as a positive expression of trust in God rather than living in theological doubt.

the scriptural conversation initiated by the book of Esther is not picked up. There are obvious reasons for this, not least that the pattern of salvation wrought in Jesus' life, death and resurrection makes clear God's involvement. Nevertheless, Jesus' story is itself placed within the larger story of Israel, and when we speak of him being the fulfilment of the Old Testament we mean the whole of it, not simply the isolated texts frequently read at Christmas and Easter. The book of Esther fits into this story, affirming God's commitment to his people, a commitment that finds its fulfilment in Jesus.[63] As Christians, therefore, we read Esther from this side of the cross, but like the Jews in Persia we do so within an ambiguous world, especially in the West, where the phenomenon of post-Christendom means that the fundamental dialogues with which we exist no longer start from the assumption of belief in the God revealed to us in the Old and New Testaments. The gospel thus fulfils the story of Esther and provides us with an additional dialogue partner from which to affirm God's saving purpose, a saving purpose that is richer than that Esther imagines. But this dialogue must work two ways. God's saving purpose, indeed the identity of the people of God, is greater than the book of Esther imagines. But Esther also asks us to ponder both how we continue to see God's saving work this side of the cross and what part we can play within this ongoing story.

---

[63] On this matter, see especially B. G. Webb, *Five Festal Garments: Christian Reflections on the Song of Songs, Ruth, Lamentations, Ecclesiastes and Esther* (Leicester: Apollos, 2000), pp. 128–133.

1:1–22
1. Some parties and their aftermath

Every story needs its starting point, but that of Esther is slightly surprising given that King Ahasuerus is the only character in it who appears later in the book. It might seem, therefore, almost to function like the extended action sequence with which most James Bond films commence – lots of absurd action but not much of relevance to the rest of the plot. But just as those sequences in the Bond films indicate 007's ability to survive seemingly impossible circumstances and characterise him in ways that prepare for the main story, so also this chapter prepares us for the oddities of the Persian court. Here, we are introduced to lavish parties and a host of activities and statements that are all meant to demonstrate the incomparable power and wealth of King Ahasuerus and all his court associates. But it is a portrayal of power which at the same time pokes fun at it by means of satire, such that anyone with an irony-deficiency needs to have it addressed before they proceed further. The king claims great power, but will turn out to be powerless in the matter of convincing his wife to come to the party. Indeed, he is not only powerless; he is a bumbling buffoon who is surrounded by sycophants who convert a trivial domestic dispute into a state emergency.

Although the book only reveals its own perspective gradually, those who heard and read it could be in no doubt of its position. God is never mentioned, but by showing the futility of such grandiose claims of human power, it opens up the question of where power really lies. The answer to that, too, will only be revealed gradually and never explicitly. But if the greatest human power turns out to be a charade, then already there is a hint that real power lies elsewhere. Just as Christian discipleship in our journey towards the heavenly dwelling is a matter of walking by faith and not by sight,[1] so also this text encourages the community of God's people to continue to trust him, even where his work is not explicit.

1. Three parties (1:1–9)

a. The imperial party (1:1–4)

Because it is important that we gain a picture of the power of Ahasuerus, the narrative begins by describing him in as elevated a manner as possible. The narrator looks back on his time, though one cannot tell from this comment how much later the book is written. The crucial point is that we look back to him as a powerful figure. This is probably why he is described as reigning over 127 provinces (Daniel 6:1 mentions 120) rather than the twenty satrapies to which Herodotus[2] refers – the provinces are smaller regions but the number becomes much larger and therefore seems more impressive. But the extent of his realm is still significant, covering 'India to Cush', or in modern terms roughly southern Pakistan to northern Sudan. At the time, it was the greatest empire ever known.[3]

But the narrator does not want to tell any tale about Ahasuerus. Rather, we focus on events in the third year of his reign (483 BC) whilst he was at Susa. Although some translations call it the 'capital' (e.g. ESV), it is more likely that the reference is to the citadel (NRSV), the fortified section of the city where Darius had built the Persian palace. It is in this part of the city where much of the book's action takes place, though we step out of its boundaries from time to time to enter the city proper. Susa was one of four royal cities employed by the Persians, being used as the king's winter residence and also as the administrative capital, which is consistent with its portrayal as the place from which royal edicts are issued.[4] Here, in the heart of his administration, Ahasuerus gave a great feast for all his officials, one lasting a full 180 days. The importance of this feast is shown by the fact that the army of Persia and Media and the prominent citizens and governors of the provinces were all in attendance. In practice, it is likely that such a feast would have had a rolling attendance with certain groups present at certain times, but the narrator is concerned that we realise the incredible extravagance

---

[1] 2 Cor. 5:7.
[2] 3.89.
[3] C. A. Moore, *Esther* (Garden City: Doubleday, 1971), p. 4, notes one of Ahasuerus's (Xerxes's) own inscriptions which claims the same realm.
[4] 1:22; 2:2–4; 3:12–15; 8:9–14; 9:14, 20–22, 29–31.

associated with this extended feast. Feasts, indeed, are a major theme in the book,[5] and the main story both begins and ends with one.[6] But the term used for *feast* throughout is one associated with drinking, which may suggest that it is more of a drunken party. Rather like the old May Day parades where the tanks and guns were paraded past the leaders of the former Soviet Union, this is both a massive celebration and a declaration of power. But like the rich fool in Jesus' parable,[7] it points to someone whose understanding of wealth and power is misplaced, not least because it was this same army that would shortly be humiliated by the Spartans at Thermopylae. Like the fool in Jesus' parable, Ahasuerus could not depend on his wealth and power.

b. The palace party (1:5–8)

With the great feast finished one might think that Ahasuerus would have had enough, but he seems to spend much of the book working on the theory that the best way to avoid a hangover is to stay drunk. Accordingly, he proceeded to give another, though smaller, feast for the next week for all those present in the citadel. Perhaps it was also a way of thanking them for their involvement in the great feast, though Reid[8] (following LXX) wonders if it might be celebrating his marriage to Vashti. However, we are given no specific clues as to the reason for the feast (as indeed for the first one) because the goal is to show Ahasuerus' excesses. Conspicuous consumption was not an invention of modernity.

This second party was given in the palace garden, which is consistent with the fact that the Persian palaces were typically surrounded by extensive gardens.[9] The extravagance of this party is evident from the description given of the grounds with its extensive and expensive hangings, furnishings and decorations. The exact translation of many of the features of verse 6 is uncertain, but it is clear that they are all expensive, and all help to announce Ahasuerus' importance even as he offers hospitality to those present. The undertone of the royal claim of power through hospitality becomes explicit in the description of the drinking at the feast. Drinks were

[5] And were also a well-known feature of Persian life – cf. A. Berlin, *Esther: The Traditional Hebrew Text with the New JPS Translation* (Philiadelphia: Jewish Publication Society, 2001), p. 4, for examples.

[6] 9:19.

[7] Luke 12:16–21.

[8] D. Reid, *Esther: An Introduction and Commentary* (Nottingham: IVP, 2008), p. 65. AT claims it celebrated his deliverance.

[9] F. Bush, *Ruth/Esther* (Dallas: Word, 1996), p. 347.

provided in the finest vessels and the wine was served in abundance because of the king's largesse. But the drinking was also done under edict from the king, which was that there was to be no compulsion, with the order given to those attending that everyone could drink as they wished. This introduces the theme of the odd ways in which Persian law operates,[10] but as Clines wryly observes, 'In an autocracy, even the absence of a rule requires a decree!'[11] The book of Esther knows that power can be used to serve the people, and it ends with Mordecai doing exactly that.[12] But it also knows that even though it sometimes appears to offer something valuable, power can be so self-serving that it becomes a grotesque parody of itself. In part, at least, it is because of Jesus' awareness of this that he calls for Christian leaders to follow his own model and be slaves of all.[13]

c. Vashti's party (1:9)

Whilst Ahasuerus was holding the palace party, Queen Vashti was holding one elsewhere in the palace for the women. It is noteworthy that, after the attention given to the excesses of Ahasuerus' parties, we are given almost no details for this one. Was it also an excessive time of drinking, a declaration of the glories of Persia? Or was it a quieter, more dignified affair? We do not know. But we are meant to notice that although Vashti gave the party for the women in the palace, it is again said that the palace belonged to Ahasuerus. Whatever Vashti's exact position and however impressive her party might have been, it too was meant to point to the glory of Ahasuerus whose authority stood behind her. Although here stated more subtly, we again see the problem of unchecked power serving only its own interests.

2. Queen Vashti's refusal (1:10–12)

Although we have had many events described, the narrative proper begins only now. In doing so, it shows that for all the grandness of his public presentation, Ahasuerus cannot affect what matters most. He cannot ensure that everyone does what he wants, and the balloon of his prestige which had been so carefully established is pricked by a woman who will not come to his party. The careful repetition of royal language in this section only serves to drive this

[10] T. S. Laniak, 'Esther', in L. C. Allen and T. S. Laniak, *Ezra, Nehemiah, Esther* (Peabody: Hendrickson, 2003), p. 195.
[11] D. J. A. Clines, *Ezra, Nehemiah, Esther* (Grand Rapids: Eerdmans, 1984), p. 278.
[12] 10:3.
[13] Mark 10:42–45.

point home, as does the careful naming of the king's servants. It is the language of power and the presence of seven servants (perhaps not strictly eunuchs) who can be named only supports this, though the book likes to name as many people as possible.

Ahasuerus' second party had run for seven days, and since it was largely a time of drinking it is no surprise that his heart was *merry with wine*. But such a statement alludes to two previous instances of powerful people whose hearts were also merry with wine before coming to a sticky end. Nabal[14] was a powerful man in the south of Judah while David was on the run from Saul. David had protected his men during sheep shearing, something necessary because of the bandits, but Nabal refused to allow David and his men to join his celebratory feast. David was only prevented from killing Nabal by the intervention of his wife Abigail. Nabal thought he had seen David off but while he was holding a feast[15] like a king, his heart also was merry from his drinking. Abigail waited until the following day to tell him she had helped David, and shortly after, Yahweh struck Nabal down. Later, David's son Amnon had raped his half-sister Tamar,[16] incurring the enmity of Tamar's brother Absalom. Absalom, personifying the idea that revenge is a dish best served cold, waited two years and then invited all his brothers to a feast after shearing his sheep. There he commanded his servants to wait until Amnon's heart was 'merry with wine'[17] and then kill him. Both stories graphically illustrate the dangers of drunkenness, and although Ahasuerus' fall will not be as dramatic he is another who makes a foolish decision because of drunkenness. Christians have taken different positions on whether or not is appropriate to drink alcohol at all, and some texts seem to take a positive attitude towards it in moderation,[18] but the Bible is clear that drunkenness is never acceptable.[19]

Unlike Nabal and Amnon, Ahasuerus loses only his prestige. On the seventh day of the feast he directed his seven servants to bring Queen Vashti, specifying that she should wear the royal crown, in order to show off her beauty to those gathered. Yet in doing so, Ahasuerus reveals his attitude to his wife. She is not someone to be honoured and loved,[20] but merely the most attractive of his possessions to display before those gathered. Instead of being joined

[14] 1 Sam. 25.
[15] 1 Sam. 25:36. As with the feasts of Esther, largely a time of drinking.
[16] 2 Sam. 13:1–21.
[17] 2 Sam. 13:28.
[18] Ps. 104:15.
[19] Prov. 20:1; 23:29–35; 31:4–7; Rom. 13:13; Gal. 5:21.
[20] Cf. Eph. 5:28.

to her as a committed covenant partner,[21] Ahasuerus treats his wife as one more object that will bring him prestige because he is married to this great beauty.[22] But for all his preening, Ahasuerus is one more drunk to fall. Vashti refuses to come. We are not told why, perhaps because telling us of her motivation would distract from the narrator's theme. All we need to know is that for all he appears to be flush with power, Ahasuerus cannot simply do as he wishes. Sending a command by his servants cannot make the queen come. His façade of power is shown for the hollow thing that it is simply because his wife will not come to the party. Vashti's refusal hints at her own dignity. But it is a crushing blow to Ahasuerus. All he can do is rage, but this is the rage of powerlessness, the frustration of those who cannot do as they wish – always a danger with kings.[23]

3. The royal council (1:13–22)

Vashti's refusal triggers a range of events, all of which serve to show the ability of a wounded ego to respond in ways that are completely out of proportion to what has happened. Ahasuerus has thrown lavish parties, so we should not be surprised that he does nothing by half-measures. Yet even as the king tries to repair his public prestige, the narrator cannot resist demonstrating that these attempts show how helpless he really is.

We are probably to assume that Ahasuerus acted immediately after Vashti's refusal, following his usual custom in consulting his advisers. Indeed, it is notable that throughout the book he does nothing without someone's advice. Kings may be meant to provide true justice and search out what is hidden,[24] but this is clearly not Ahasuerus' strong suit. Yet in itself this may be one of the ways in which the book points to God's unseen activity, since even kings are ultimately under God's control.[25] Ahasuerus' actions will frequently be foolish indeed, yet God's unseen providence may be hidden in his incessant need for counsel.

But there is also a strong sense of parody here. The king is said to have consulted his wise men who *knew the times* and were versed in legal matters. It is the law that will be crucial, though it is notable that the word used for law (*dāt*) is specific to the Persian period. The

---

[21] Mal. 2:14–15.

[22] Some rabbinic texts (B. *Megillah* 12b) suggest Vashti was to come naked, though there is nothing here to require that. Cf. J. Carruthers, *Esther through the Ages* (Oxford: Blackwell, 2008), pp. 62–64.

[23] Prov. 19:12.

[24] Prov. 16:10; 25:1.

[25] Prov. 21:1.

law they discuss is not Israel's law, something that is central to Haman's deception when he arranges for the destruction of the Jews.[26] There may be an echo here of the men of Issachar who came to see David after he became king because they had understanding of the times and knew what Israel ought to do[27] – but, if so, it is only to show how little these men really knew in comparison. Just as the king had seven attendants who were named when he sent for Vashti, so also he has seven advisers whose names are also given. Of the seven, Memucan is mentioned last but appears to be the senior figure since he speaks on behalf of the group. As well as being wise, we are also told that they were from the princes of the kingdom, and thus those whose own prosperity depends upon that of the king. Self-interest may thus prevent them from actually offering wise advice.

It is not uncommon for the powerful to use the law to their own ends, and Ahasuerus is certainly typical. Confronted by Vashti's refusal to come to his party he asks his advisers a specifically legal question. What, according to the law, is to be done to Vashti because of her failure to carry out the king's command, especially one delivered with such splendour as this when seven attendants were sent? There was, of course, no law that specifically addressed the problem of a queen not attending the king's party, but the problem for Ahasuerus is that she has disobeyed him. Yet showing the effects of too much wine, he magnifies a simple domestic dispute into a state crisis, a matter for law to consider. Ahasuerus has no sense of proportion in all this because his ego has been wounded, and Vashti's refusal has shown how fragile his power really is. The only possible response from his perspective is to restore the façade and show how great his power is.

Confronted by a legal question, Memucan responded on behalf of the advisers. It is notable that he does not challenge Ahasuerus' basic presupposition. The king has asked a legal question, and the loyal servant must provide a legal answer, even when it means that the law becomes a mockery of itself. Moreover, where Ahasuerus elevated a domestic dispute into a crisis of his own authority, Memucan takes it even further, insisting that Vashti's refusal is a crisis for the whole Empire. Of course, he is astute enough to know that Vashti's refusal has no direct legal implications and he carefully sidesteps any direct legal comment. Instead, he sets up a chain of events he insists will follow on before then giving his advice. First, news of Vashti's refusal will be made known to all the other women.

---

[26] 3:8. Note that *torah* does not occur in the book of Esther.
[27] 1 Chr. 12:32 (MT 12:33).

This will in turn lead them to consider their husbands with contempt on the grounds that Vashti refused the king's command to attend the party. This feminine rebellion will begin with the women of the noble households who would begin that very day to resist the authority of their husbands, creating an abundance of contempt and wrath. It does not take long to realise that this chain is a complete straw woman, and that husbands who treated their wives with respect rather than as something to stroke their own prestige while under the effects of alcohol need fear no such thing. But Memucan and his associates breathe in the rarefied air of the palace in Susa, and the fragility of their own positions mimics that of Ahasuerus. Everything must be controlled, and even the outside possibility of ridicule (however well deserved) must be avoided. Instead of marriage being where male and female complete each other in loving commitment,[28] the Persian court thinks of it only to serve its own prestige, and that prestige is built on foundations of sand.

Having outlined the supposed implications of Vashti's refusal, Memucan then advised the king on what he should do. First, he should issue a decree barring Vashti from ever again approaching the king. This is not technically divorcing her, but ensures she remained within the harem. Both the books of Esther and Daniel indicate that Persian laws could not be repealed,[29] something which prepares for Haman's decree for the destruction of the Jews.[30] It is often suggested that this is highly improbable since empires always need the means to revoke bad laws, but it is more likely that the phrase simply means that the law could not be contravened.[31] The seriousness with which Vashti's refusal was treated was thus to be evidenced by a law that would prevent even the king from taking her back. Vashti would then be replaced by another who was better than her. We are not told how this alternative woman would be better, though presumably she was meant to be obedient to her husband in all things. Memucan concluded his advice by insisting that this process would ensure that all women throughout the Empire would honour their husbands, no matter what their social position.

Memucan's advice is as ripe with folly as his suggested chain of events that would follow news of Vashti's refusal, because every attempt at shoring up power and prestige that does not really exist simply shows how vacuous it is. The length of his speech simply

[28] Gen. 2:18–25.
[29] Esth. 8:8; Dan. 6:9, 13, 16, though the phrasing in Esth. 8:8 is different.
[30] 3:12–15.
[31] Berlin, *Esther*, p. 18.

gives more opportunity for his folly to become evident.[32] It does not occur to him that there is no better way of ensuring that all the women hear about Vashti's actions than putting it into an official decree that everyone is supposed to know.[33] But more than that, by insisting that Vashti be replaced by someone else, he creates the context by which Esther will rise to the throne. Esther will be a model of obedience, and yet she is the one who will achieve her goals above those of Ahasuerus. Whoever reads this story can also see here one of those places where God is at work. Haman's attempt to destroy the Jews will require someone inside the palace to thwart it, and Esther will rise to power at the right time for this to happen, though she will also use all her wits and skill to do so. The greater irony of Memucan's proposal is thus not that he actually promotes Vashti's actions, but rather that he shows how powerless he really is before God. Often in the book of Esther, and so much of life, it is in the gaps behind the ironies that we see God quietly at work.

Just as the chapter began with a display of royal power, so it ends with all the resources of the Empire put into the issue of the decree. In what becomes a frequent motif in the book, Ahasuerus was pleased by the advice he received, and so acted on it. Thus, the scribes were summoned to write out the decree in each of the languages and scripts of the Empire to ensure that every man would rule in his household. The last part of verse 22 is unfortunately obscure,[34] but seems to indicate that evidence for the husband's authority would be seen in the language spoken in the home being that of the man, something that could be a difficulty in a multi-ethnic Empire.[35] It is rather doubtful that any human decree could achieve this, but Ahasuerus cannot distinguish between the politics of the Empire and choices that individual families would need to make about the best language to use. After all, what would be done in households where both husband and wife used a second language or one where one partner did not know the home language of the other? This problem is faced by many households in the world today, and each will resolve it differently. But Ahasuerus does not see marriage as something where partners negotiate the best path out of loving commitment to one another and so chooses to stress his authority through his decree. His problem is that by the end of this chapter we know that in reality he has very little power, and there have been enough hints already that real power lies elsewhere in an unseen providence, though it does not stop Ahasuerus from

[32] Eccl. 10:14.
[33] Clines. *Ezra, Nehemiah, Esther*, p. 33.
[34] It is absent from LXX, hence NRSV.
[35] Cf. Neh. 13:23–24.

easily abusing the power he has. What that might mean is not yet explored; at this stage it is only necessary that believers know that the script of empire and its grandeur can be read against the official spin. And that is enough to lead us to see what that different reading might be.

Through its integrated use of Scripture and satire, this chapter models something very important for contemporary Christians. Almost all news items come to us with some form of spin, some attempt to control how we view it. A whole host of consultants have emerged to become 'spin doctors' for those in power, controlling how we receive information about people and events. This is not restricted to politics, of course, and can even become part of discourse within the church, but politics is perhaps the most obvious place to see it. However, we should not think that this chapter's concerns in contemporary society should be limited to politics – an equally pressing concern might also be with the subtle and not so subtle advocacy of consumerism that confronts us so regularly. Advertisers tell us 'Just do it' or 'You're worth it', encouraging an individualist view of life that is contrary to the central place of community within the biblical text. The curiosity of this is that political discourse tends to speak of the importance of building community whilst simultaneously supporting a consumerist approach to life.

One response to observing such control of information (and its internal contradictions) is simply to mock it, and this approach has provided fodder for comedians who look to make topical comment. Such mockery can have a positive intent, but often it is content simply to note the foibles and follies of those in power. This chapter certainly does that through its satirical presentation of Ahasuerus' Persia and his political systems. But it does more, and it is the extra element that is crucial. At crucial points, the satire here deliberately refers us to other passages of Scripture. For example, Ahasuerus' drunken decision to summon Vashti is intended to point us to the foolish actions of Nabal in 1 Samuel 25 and Amnon in 2 Samuel 13. Memucan's lengthy speech becomes an example of the folly against which we are warned in Ecclesiastes 10:14. It is not simply that we can see parallels to these texts. Rather, the book of Esther encourages us to read this satire through the prism of a range of scriptural references. In doing so, it provides a constructive model for addressing a society that does not necessarily recognise the right of those who speak for God to be heard. Here, Scripture is introduced to public discourse, not by endless quoting of chapter and verse in a way that outsiders would find off-putting, but by integrating it into a satire that invites all to participate. Its satire highlights the errors of its society, while offering a positive alternative for those who are prepared to hear the options it offers. It provides a framework that shows the failings of the Persian structure while also initiating a conversation that, because it is shaped by Scripture, offers something more. It is not the only model for dealing with a world where practising Christians are frequently a minority voice, but it provides an important alternative for us – challenging us both to a better knowledge of Scripture and to engage willingly with our world employing it.

2:1–23
2. Providence in the passive voice

Since the study of grammar does not rank highly on the priorities of many today the subtlety of the biblical narrative is often missed precisely because so much depends upon the care with which the words are chosen. This chapter is a case in point. In a book which never mentions God directly it is necessary to find other ways of referring to his presence and activity, usually in an understated way. One method which had become quite popular by the time of the New Testament was using what is known as the divine passive. This technique allowed someone to refer to God's actions without naming him directly. Thus, when James and John asked Jesus for exalted positions in the kingdom, Jesus responded that they were not his to give but belonged to those 'for whom it has been prepared'.[1] Jesus clearly means that only God can give honour in the Kingdom, but by using a passive form he leaves it for the hearer to realise this. This technique did not originate in the New Testament, and is clearly present in this chapter. It is noticeable that there are important collections of passive verbs associated with both Esther and Mordecai in their dealings with the Persians, verbs that do not directly tell us who is acting. Alternatively, Esther finds favour without it being said that she looked for it. Such silences could be nothing more than a polite way of saying 'This is what happens with the Persians,' but the things which happen have implications for events later in the book. They leave open the possibility that what initially seems like the outcome of Persian processes may actually point to God's providential care of his people, though like much providence it can only be recognised when we look back on it. But there is something else to note, and that is that the Jews mentioned in this chapter are also actively working for the welfare of others.

[1] Mark 10:40.

Perhaps there is a hint that providence is most active in those whose lives are shaped by God's own concerns.

1. A study in contrasts (2:1–7)

a. The quest for Miss Persia? (2:1–4)

Some time later, Ahasuerus's anger subsided. How much later is not made clear, but when it did he remembered Vashti. When God remembers someone in the Old Testament it is often a sign that he is about to act graciously towards them,[2] but Ahasuerus is caught by his own decree. He can remember what Vashti did and what was decreed against her, but he is unable to act. He is like the penitent drunk who wishes that certain decisions had not been made under the influence of alcohol, but cannot undo what has been done. In any case, he is caught by the power of his own immovable decree,[3] and though he can remember Vashti, and perhaps even wish he had acted otherwise, he does not act.

One of Ahasuerus' key characteristics is that he almost never acts on his own initiative but only on the advice of another. Whereas Vashti's refusal to attend the party had triggered a pseudo-legal problem for which he could request advice,[4] no such option exists here because the problem was triggered by his own decree. But though Ahasuerus makes no request, those attending him were aware of the problem. The queen had been removed from office and another was needed. So a group of the lads attending Ahasuerus offered their advice.[5] These may be the same ones who later advise the king concerning Mordecai's reward[6] but the important point is that they are probably younger men, and their advice may reflect their own interests. Their plan is simple, though it takes the conspicuous consumption of Ahasuerus' parties in chapter 1 to a new level. In short, the king needed a queen and the best way to find one was to gather every beautiful virgin[7] in the Empire to Susa. Whoever pleased the king would be the new queen. There is an obvious parallel here with the aged David's appointment of Abishag, except that text makes clear that she was the only one

[2] Gen. 8:1; Exod. 2:24.

[3] 1:19–22.

[4] 1:15.

[5] The description of these servants is remarkably similar to that of Samuel in 1 Sam. 3:1. If the parallel is intentional then it is probably only to parody them.

[6] 6:3, 5.

[7] There is debate as to whether biblical Hebrew has a word that specifically means 'virgin'. But since the girls here had to be marriageable it is difficult to avoid the conclusion that virginity was necessary.

brought in and he had no sexual relationship with her.[8] Even when the Persians mirror Israel's practices, they show how wrong they get it.

Finding a queen thus requires massive expenditure, with officers appointed in all 127 provinces to locate every beautiful virgin and ensure their delivery to Susa. Once there, they would be placed in the care of the keeper of the harem, a eunuch named Hegai, and would receive an extensive regime of beauty treatments.[9] Many children's Bibles and the like portray this as a beauty contest, but beauty is only the entry requirement. Since the means by which a woman pleases the king involves spending the night with him after the beauty treatments are concluded,[10] we can reasonably assume that good conversation was not on anyone's mind. The suggestion is an appalling abuse of many women who, though notionally some form of concubine in the harem, will be denied a life of their own, whilst taking so many women from the provinces denies local men a chance at marriage. Without denying the importance of single people in churches today, it is clear that the Old Testament regards marriage as the normal condition for adults.[11] But this proposal sets aside the possibility of marriage for many simply to provide one man's pleasure – a particularly ironic abuse of family life given Memucan's supposed support of it.[12] Yet, Ahasuerus is again pleased by this proposal, so the wheels of Persian bureaucracy grind into action for his pleasure.

b. Mordecai and Esther (2:5–7)

In marked contrast to Ahasuerus' excesses, we are now introduced to a Jewish family living in the Diaspora. Although Babylon's fall in 538 BC had allowed exiles to return to their homeland, many had taken seriously the advice to settle where they were and contribute positively to it.[13] Among them was one who lived in the citadel area of Susa named Mordecai. If we can identify him with a palace accountant mentioned in some texts from the time,[14] then the citadel is where we would expect him. But even if this is not the case he is clearly an important person. This is evident from his lengthy

[8] 1 Kgs 1:1–4.
[9] 2:12.
[10] 2:12–15.
[11] Gen. 2:24.
[12] 1:17–18, cf. L. M. Day, *Esther* (Nashville: Abingdon, 2005), p. 41.
[13] Jer. 29:4–23.
[14] This is not impossible but by no means certain. Cf. D. G. Firth, 'The Third Quest for the Historical Mordecai and the Genre of the Book of Esther', *Old Testament Essays* 16 (2003), pp. 236–242.

genealogy, tracing his family back to one Kish who had been exiled with Jehoiachin when Nebuchadnezzar first captured Jerusalem in 597 BC.[15] Mordecai's name is Babylonian ('man of Marduk', thus associated with the chief Babylonian deity), but it is not impossible that he also had a Jewish name that has not been recorded, as is the case with Esther herself. Mordecai's genealogy is similar to Saul's,[16] and though not significant yet it becomes a feature in chapter 3 when Haman is introduced.

Where Ahasuerus, and the palace generally, is noted for conspicuous consumption, Mordecai is a model of moderation and care. Where Ahasuerus spends for his own satisfaction, Mordecai reflects God's concern for the weak by raising his orphaned cousin.[17] Although better known by her Babylonian name of Esther, she is first introduced by her Hebrew name of Hadassah ('Myrtle') to ensure we know that her roots are thoroughly Jewish. But having been told of her lack of family, we are then told of her beauty. Esther's beauty is emphasised by mentioning it twice, and the second time matches the terms set for the women to be gathered to the royal household. Beauty in the Old Testament frequently catches people's attention, though with Saul[18] and Absalom[19] their attractiveness led people astray. But for Esther, in spite of the care given by her cousin, beauty was dangerous because it exposed her to the interest of the king's men.

2. Esther becomes queen (2:8–18)

a. Esther's arrival in the harem (2:8–11)

Mordecai had taken Esther to a place of seeming security, but she would soon be taken to a place where she needed to discover that security for herself. So, when the king's command was published, Esther found herself with many other virgins, taken to the palace to be cared for by Hegai. None of these girls is said to go by their own choice because although palace life might seem desirable, becoming a concubine in the harem was not the stuff of fairy tales. And Esther

[15] 2 Kgs 24:10 – 17. It is sometimes objected that the grammar makes more sense if Mordecai was the one exiled (e.g. L. B. Paton, *A Critical and Exegetical Commentary on the Book of Esther* [Edinburgh: T & T Clark, 1908], p. 167), but the book's narrative skill does not prevent some awkward phrases slipping through, and since Mordecai can be the subject we should give preference to a reading giving sense over nonsense.

[16] 1 Sam. 9:1.

[17] Exod. 22:22; Deut. 10:18; 14:29; 16:11, 14; 24:17, 19–21; 26:12–13; 27:19.

[18] 1 Sam. 9:2.

[19] 2 Sam. 14:25.

is among those taken. There is perhaps a hint of force in her case – the others were assembled, but Esther is taken, though the point should not be stressed. The result for them all was the same though. They lost their freedom and were kept by Hegai in the harem. That Esther makes the most of a bad situation does not make it any better.[20]

Whatever differences might have been present in how the girls came to the harem, there is something decisively different in Esther's experience there. We are not told what she did beyond continuing to obey her guardian, but the narrator introduces a key theme that occurs throughout the book. Esther gains favour with Hegai.[21] She later gains favour with Ahasuerus,[22] and when the Jews are threatened uses it as the basis for her appeals to him.[23] This favour is vitally important, a clue to God's presence in the story, though for the moment it appears unobtrusively as the basis for Hegai improving her lot within the harem. He ensures her access to the beauty treatments and food as well as giving her seven superior attendants and transferring her to the best place in the harem. Esther neither sought entry to the harem nor advancement within it, yet both came to her. The one thing we are told she has done is remain obedient to Mordecai in not revealing her ethnicity. No reason is given for this and we have not yet been told of significant anti-Jewish sentiment, but it would almost certainly have meant accepting that she could not retain a kosher lifestyle. Life outside of a controllable Jewish context meant making decisions about how to live in a way that was true to the intention of such matters even if traditional forms could not be followed, just as Christians in many parts of the world today have to make decisions about how they practise their faith in an environment that might be hostile to it. But her faithfulness in keeping silent is clearly important as Mordecai daily wandered around the gate area seeking information about Esther's welfare. Already, it is evident that God's people have different priorities to the Persian aristocracy. Concern for the weak does not end once it becomes difficult for Mordecai. Neither does Esther abandon obedience to her guardian once he can no longer supervise her. Both continue to act as they should, and in the midst

---

[20] C. M. Bechtel, *Esther* (Louisville: Westminster John Knox, 2002), p. 31.

[21] Some (e.g. S. W. Crawford, 'Esther', in L. E. Keck [ed.], *The New Interpreter's Bible*, vol. 3 [Nashville: Abingdon, 1999], p. 888) suggest that gaining favour implies effort by Esther, but there is nothing to suggest that this phrase differs from the more common 'finding favour', and is probably an idiom reflecting an engaging personality on Esther's part.

[22] 2:17; 5:2.

[23] 5:8; 7:3; 8:5.

of this the favour Esther finds points to a greater purpose being worked out.

b. Esther's promotion (2:12–18)

Having demonstrated the faithfulness of Mordecai and Esther, the narrative returns to life in the harem with a general description of the process followed by each girl, again showing the massive waste built into the system, waste that contrasts markedly with the pattern established by Mordecai and Esther. Each received a full twelve-month beauty programme made up of six months of oil of myrrh and six months of cosmetic treatments, a process so important that it too was according to royal edict. Before their night with the king the women could take whatever they wanted with them in their attempt to please the king. And it was a night on which much depended, because if they did not please him sufficiently then all that remained was life as a concubine, trapped in the palace in another part of the harem and waiting only for the king to summon them back. The description is also full of *double entendre*. The verb 'to go' (*bō'*) occurs five times in various forms in 2:12–14. Although it can simply describe a journey someone might make, it is also a euphemism for sexual activity,[24] hinting again at the realities behind the process by which the new queen was to be selected.

With the general pattern established, we return to Esther so her story and that of the other women merge. From the perspective of the Empire, Esther is simply one more beautiful virgin that the king will deflower,[25] but the narrator imbues her with special honour in two remarkable ways. First, she is placed in her own social context. She is not just anyone, but the daughter of Abihail. We do not know of him from elsewhere, but this touch stresses her family, something the Empire cannot take away. This is also made clear because Mordecai's adoption of her is again mentioned. Her place in the harem means the king will claim her, but he cannot take away the care and concern of her community. Second, we are again told of Esther's knack of gaining favour. She previously found favour with Hegai, but now we discover that it happened with all who met her. Again, nothing is said to indicate why this happens, but it is a vital element in her experience, hinting that something better may await her. Yet, there may also be no need to say why she continues to gain

[24] 2 Sam. 11:4.
[25] A. M. Rodriguez, *Esther: A Theological Approach* (Berrien Springs: Andrews University Press, 1995), pp. 66–68, goes to great lengths to claim that in Esther's case there was no attempt to establish sexual compatibility, but there is nothing to suggest that anything other than the normal pattern for her.

favour, for everything we are told about her shows that she, like Mordecai, has made God's priorities her own. Psalm 15:5 makes clear that such a person will 'never be shaken' (NIV). Esther's experience demonstrates the reality of this whilst making clear that believers still pass through times of difficult trial. Rather, as Esther continues to stand within the community of God's people and follow their patterns within a painful personal experience, so she continues to find favour.

The contrast with Persian sensibilities is underlined by events when Esther's turn to go into the king came around. She too had the opportunity to take whatever she wanted, but rather than claiming things for herself she simply accepted Hegai's advice. Esther takes only what Hegai suggests, but she is then taken to the king. It is not something over which she has any control. But before we hear the outcome of Esther's visit to the king, we are given a brief chrono-logical note, which is that Esther was taken to the palace in the tenth month of the seventh year of Ahasuerus' reign, some four years after Vashti had been deposed. This may suggest the enormity and wastefulness of Ahasuerus' search, though of course the twelve-month beauty regime meant that the visits to him could not have started immediately. It is also worth noting however that this was the same period as Herodotus indicates he was busy losing his wars against the Greeks, most notably his struggle against the Spartan king Leonidas at Thermopylae and then the decisive defeats at Salamis and Plataea. The tenth month is mid-winter, cold and wet even in Susa,[26] so it was hardly propitious timing for Esther. Even allowing for Ahasuerus' military distractions, Esther is hardly the first candidate. So, outwardly it seemed that Esther had little more chance than the many that preceded her. And yet, we are told the king loved her more than all the women, and that she gained grace and favour with him, more than all the virgins. Yet again, the narrative hints here at something more. Esther has done nothing other than act as a responsible girl should when forced into concubinage. But just as she found favour with all before, so she finds grace and favour with Ahasuerus, and this distinguishes her from all others. The narrative does not thereby suggest that God's care for his people means they avoid pain and suffering, for none would choose her position. But it does indicate that even in bleak situations, God's providential care is operative, and the promise of Psalm 15:5, that those who make God's priorities their own will not be shaken, continues to be true. Perhaps more importantly, it is true in a more profound way than those might imagine who think God's

[26] 'Tebeth' means 'mud'.

providential care prevents suffering. Esther does not give voice to her suffering in the same way as Job or the poet of Psalm 73, but her circumstances are given additional richness when read in light of these texts.

With Esther as the end of his quest, Ahasuerus then set the crown on Esther's head and made her queen in place of Vashti. Vashi had refused to come to the earlier party wearing the crown, so now it is given to Esther. Ahasuerus then promptly returned to type, throwing another great party for his officials and attendants, this one known as Esther's feast, to celebrate. He also invited all the provinces to join the celebrations, perhaps through the granting of a holiday (though some form of tax relief is possible[27]) and the sharing of gifts. Everyone is called to celebrate the new queen's arrival, though none knew how important her Jewish identity was, the one thing Ahasuerus definitely did not know about her.

3. Discovery of a plot against the king (2:19–23)

One might think that Esther's promotion would end the introductory section of the book, but there is one more vignette, the importance of which does not become evident until 6:1–13. As with Esther's promotion, it makes careful use of passives to show how Mordecai's faithful activity saves the king's life. It begins with a curious note about the virgins being gathered a second time, which is awkward because there is no specific reference to a first gathering.[28] But Gordis' suggestion makes sense – the virgins not brought before the king were gathered so they could be sent back home, with the first gathering hinted at by 2:8.[29] The other key note is that Mordecai was sitting in the king's gate. The gate was a substantial area, and Mordecai's presence there may indicate that he was already some sort of official since the gate was used by officials, though this is not yet made explicit.[30] While the virgins were gathered for their dismissal, Esther remained in the palace. Again, her obedience to Mordecai is stressed. Following his command as she had always done, she had not revealed her ethnic background and family. She is queen, but faithful obedience remains. By mentioning her obedience on this matter a second time, the narrator also prepares for Haman's marked anti-Jewish sentiments in chapter 3. For now, we do not know of the threat, but the need for Esther's

---

[27] F. Bush, *Ruth/Esther* (Dallas: Word, 1996), p. 358.

[28] LXX omits this statement, whilst AT relocates it.

[29] R. Gordis, 'Studies in the Esther Narrative', *Journal of Biblical Literature* 95 (1976), p. 47.

[30] Cf. 3:2–3.

continuing silence indicates that at least something was already there.

Having established where Esther and Mordecai were, we learn of a plot to kill Ahasuerus. Ahasuerus was eventually killed by some of his officers, but this plot involved two attendants named Bigthana and Teresh who were angered in some way. As threshold guards they might be able to kill him as he passed by, but if they were to escape they would need other support or else Ahasuerus' other guards would kill them.[31] How far their conspiracy went is not recorded, but at some stage someone spoke about it. And information about their plot was made known to Mordecai. The passive verb means we do not know who told him while suggesting it was not information he sought. Mordecai simply sought to be faithful to Esther while seated in the gate, perhaps while carrying out his normal employment. But this information was revealed to him and he passed it on to her.[32] Exactly how he would have done so is not stated, but he is later able to communicate through another palace eunuch.[33] Mordecai is not seeking promotion, but he remains faithful to the state in spite of the dangers it poses to him. Once the information reached Esther, she passed it on for investigation, resulting in both men's execution. Although most versions say they were hanged, it is more likely that they were impaled on a stake.[34] As long as their fundamental existence and faith are not challenged, both Mordecai and Esther can live as model citizens, though the limits to this will soon become apparent. But the principle that this is at least possible for believers, even in a fairly oppressive state, is established.

As well as this, the whole affair was recorded in the Books of the Chronicles of Persia before the king. Here, though, we come to an abrupt halt. Persian kings were noted for richly rewarding those who helped them, so once the events were recorded we expect a reward to be noted. Instead, the narrative suddenly stops with this curious note. That the plot was revealed to Mordecai was clearly providential, as was Esther's promotion and uncanny knack for finding favour with all who met her. Providence seems to have brought Esther to the throne, so what has happened to Mordecai? Has he been left aside? Ending the story so abruptly here forces us to ask such questions, but it also opens up other possibilities. The

[31] That the idiom of the guards 'putting forth their hand against the king' (my translation) refers to an attempt on the king's life is clear from the parallel in 1 Sam. 26:9 where David rebukes Abishai for suggesting that he would kill Saul.

[32] Note that this is the first time she is called 'Queen Esther'.

[33] 4:5.

[34] ESV mg.

most important is to emphasise that although God's providential care is evident throughout it does not mean that the faithfulness of God's people is immediately rewarded. Mordecai and Esther must continue to be faithful, but they cannot know that the significance of their actions only becomes meaningful once all the Jews are under threat of losing their lives. We must not over-interpret everything that happens to us. But where God's concern for his people is being worked out it will become significant – we just do not know when until after it has happened. In the mean time, we are called to faithfulness, even in host cultures that may be antagonistic to faith.

This chapter does not address all the issues associated with living within an antagonistic culture and how we discern God's providence within it – that, after all, would require a somewhat different text to this. But we should understand this chapter as modelling an important approach to these questions: issues which increasingly confront Christians around the world, and which arise in a particular way for western Christians following the collapse of Christendom. Two key themes emerge, however, which are offered through this chapter as a model for how we address these issues, though without losing sight of the importance of deconstructing Persian claims to power, as was also evident in chapter 1.

The first theme is evident in Mordecai's continued concern for Esther, a concern which models not only care for the weak but a larger awareness of the importance of continuing to live out what it means to be faithful to God above all else. Paul similarly emphasised this for Christians[35] so that we understand that living for God also means sustaining those most at risk among the people of God. For western Christians, this should mean cultivating an awareness of the needs of the church throughout the world, especially given that much of the growth in Christianity worldwide is happening amongst the poor and, frequently, the oppressed in the majority world. Living in a culture which does not accept Christian values means we cannot enforce those values but it does not mean we lose sight of them in the shaping of our own discipleship. But this is tempered by the need to discern what is central – Esther could not maintain a kosher lifestyle but in this case at least she saw it within the larger context of remaining faithful to her people. In New Testament terms, that means we remain committed to the values and goals of the kingdom of God, but we need to reflect on Scripture to discern how we best do that. But the importance of keeping committed to kingdom values remains.

[35] Gal. 6:10.

Tied into this is the second key theme, which is to be aware that God continues to work in and through his people, often in ways we cannot immediately discern, and that those ways may even for a period lead us to pass through experiences we would not otherwise choose. But, and this is vital, God's providential purposes are being worked out even if they can only be seen with hindsight. But we must see this theme in light of the first. William Temple is reputed to have said, 'When I pray, coincidences happen, and when I don't, they don't.' Esther, of course, never mentions prayer, but the point is the same. It is as God's people commit themselves to God's purposes that we discern his providence at work. So, just as chapter 1 encourages us to build a worldview through Scripture that enables us to deconstruct a dominant worldview which is contrary to the gospel, so here we are encouraged to build our own lives around that same structure because it is then that we see how God is at work in us. We must just guard against the idea that what God decides to do will always make us comfortable, though arguably anyone who has built up a scripturally-informed worldview will know that anyway.

3:1–15
3. Power and corruption in high places

Esther's appointment as queen and Mordecai's ability to work in the palace gate, Susa's administrative centre, has shown that it was possible for Hebrews to function within the Persian Empire. Care was clearly needed, which is why Esther had to keep her ethnicity to herself, but it was possible to work in and for a state that was not overtly hostile to their faith. Mordecai demonstrated this by alerting the palace officials of an attempt on the king's life. Yet although this would normally lead to a rich reward, nothing more was done for him than to record this in the royal Chronicles.[1] We expect more, but cannot yet know that the failure adequately to reward Mordecai ultimately will contribute to the deliverance of the Jews. Just as God was with Joseph while enslaved in an Egyptian house,[2] leading him to find favour with his master, so God has been with both Esther as she found favour with everyone and Mordecai, even when it seems that the reward he was due has been missed.

The importance of this becomes evident in this chapter, where conflicts of interest and purpose become evident, introducing motifs that sustain the narrative until 9:19. These conflicts revolve around the question of power, and though chapter 1 has already raised fundamental questions about the effectiveness of human power, it does not mean that the characters in this story do not seek it. But chapter 1 has given us a framework through which to read human attempts at power. This chapter particularly warns about the use of power to substantiate one's own concerns rather than the people for whom power is given. All human power is ultimately limited, but those who do not set their use of power within God's reign can be

[1] 2:19–23.
[2] Gen. 39:3.

tempted to abuse it, seeking only that which serves them and not their people. Ambition and power will thus prove to be a heady mix, leading to a magnification of minor issues into major threats. This chapter insists that all such approaches to power produce only confusion and pain.

1. Conflict between Haman and Mordecai (3:1–7)

a. Haman's promotion (3:1)

Although we now begin the book's main narrative thread there is one more character to introduce. Haman will be the villain of the piece, though we do not immediately know this. A casual glance at the beginning of this chapter suggests Mordecai may have suffered a great injustice. After his name was written in the royal Chronicles and nothing more the very next point noted is Haman's elevation. But care is needed with the phrase *after these things*[3] because an important narrative element in the book of Esther is the way it gradually introduces a chronology for reading the story. According to 1:1, Vashti was deposed in Ahasuerus' third year, but Esther only became queen in his seventh year.[4] Haman will soon cast the lot to determine the opportune time to destroy the Jews and we are told that this occurred in Ahasuerus' twelfth year.[5] So Haman's promotion may not have been close to Mordecai's discovering the plot against the king. Even so, we are probably meant to be shocked by Haman's elevation above all the king's other officials. Kings, like anyone with unfettered power in a realm, always run the risk of using their power arbitrarily, promoting favourites and ignoring the genuinely able. Likewise, many who have faithfully served in a variety of roles will face the disappointment of not having their contribution recognised while others are promoted over them. We cannot generalise from Mordecai's experience, but as the story unfolds it turns out that being passed over when he should have been rewarded will be precisely the point that leads to the Jews' deliverance,[6] so we should at least allow for the possibility of God having greater purposes than we can recognise, though without insisting on it.

But there is something more troubling about Haman than just his sudden promotion, though since he is promoted from among the officials it is clear that he is already an important person. Like

[3] 3:1.
[4] 2:16.
[5] 3:7.
[6] 6:1–3.

Mordecai,[7] we are given a genealogy for Haman, a genealogy that evokes older troubles for the Jews. Haman's father Hammedatha is not otherwise known, but he is also called an *Agagite*. This almost certainly means he was descended from Agag, the Amalekite king Saul had failed to destroy as Yahweh had commanded.[8] Although many generations have passed, we are introduced to an old and simmering conflict. In many parts of the world today conflict among peoples reaches back to events hundreds of years before, and though the current generation is removed from the origins of the conflict it is expected to continue the fight. That is certainly the case here. In fact, the conflict between Israel and Amalek goes back before Saul to the exodus, as the Amalekites were the first people to oppose Israel on their way to Sinai, leading to Yahweh declaring his enmity with them.[9] But for Esther, the important conflict is that between Saul and Agag. Mordecai's genealogy had indicated an association with Saul's family; Haman's indicates that he is of the family that ultimately saw Saul lose the throne. Thus the scene is set for conflict. Can old adversaries survive, or will the fact that one has power mean that the opportunity is taken to settle old scores?

b. Mordecai refuses to honour Haman (3:2–6)

With Haman elevated, we are immediately moved to the king's gate where his officials were. As Haman passed through there the king's officials would offer him the appropriate homage, much the same as we would expect to give proper respect to dignitaries today. Indeed, the extent of this is evident in that they both *bowed down and paid homage*[10] to him. To pay homage is typically to prostrate oneself (and is also a key verb for worship in the Old Testament), though in Persia it was probably more of an exaggerated bow.[11] Yet two curious notes are highlighted. First, the king had commanded that Haman be honoured. Persian officials would typically offer respect to a senior member of the court anyway, making the command unnecessary. Ahasuerus is fond of issuing pointless commands,[12] but there may be a hint that the officials regarded Haman as

---

[7] 2:5.

[8] 1 Sam. 15:1–9, though he was subsequently put to death by Samuel (1 Sam. 15:32–33). Although Saul was meant to have destroyed them, there are sufficient other references to Amalekites (e.g. 2 Sam. 1:1–16) to indicate that some survived. See also Num. 24:7.

[9] Exod. 17:8–16.

[10] 3:2.

[11] A. Berlin,, *Esther: The Traditional Hebrew Text with the New JPS Translation* (Philadelphia: Jewish Publication Society, 2001), pp. 34–36.

[12] 1:8, 22.

unworthy.[13] Second, Mordecai did not pay the appropriate respect for Haman in spite of the royal command.

We are not told why Mordecai does not offer the necessary respect, though it has not stopped considerable speculation, most of which ends up rather puzzled because the Old Testament does not have a problem with paying appropriate respect to pagan rulers and officials.[14] All we have is the hint of the old conflict with Amalek. But our puzzlement is matched by that of the other officials who asked Mordecai directly about why he transgressed the king's command, and we should bear in mind that the book consistently restricts our vision to what the various characters can see. The officials can only see that Mordecai does not obey, but they lack the insight necessary to understand why, hence their question to him. The language of the question is revealing – they are not concerned with protocol but Mordecai's transgression of the command. Breaches of protocol might be overlooked, but transgressing the king's command could bring serious punishment. Although they did this daily, Mordecai would not listen. In effect, he refused to respond to their questions.

We are never directly told why Mordecai refused to honour Haman,[15] perhaps because doing so distracts us from the chapter's central themes. It soon becomes evident that Haman is not the only problem, and the anti-Jewish sentiment hinted at when Mordecai directed Esther not to mention her ethnicity[16] becomes more prominent in the insistent questioning of the officials. Mordecai has not answered, but they took the matter to Haman because Mordecai was Jewish. Most commentators assume Mordecai told them this, but we could perhaps translate verse 4b as 'they told Haman to see if the matter of Mordecai would stand, because it was reported to them that he was Jewish'.[17] Mordecai's actions would then be consistent with his advice to Esther while also suggesting widespread Jewish antipathy, though this is evident on the more

---

[13] J. Baldwin, *Esther: An Introduction and Commentary* (Leicester: IVP, 1984), p. 72. This is more probable than C. A. Moore, who simply regards it as necessary for the plot, in *Esther* (Garden City: Doubleday, 1971), p. 36.

[14] Gen. 42:6; Esth. 8:3.

[15] Though the AT links Haman to the conspirators of the previous chapter, whilst the LXX additions provide religious reasons.

[16] 2:10.

[17] On this translation, see P. Haupt, 'Critical Notes on Esther', *AJSL* 24 (1907–1908), p. 123. The key issue is whether the verb *higgîd* is personal ('he reported') or impersonal ('it was reported'). Normally, a different form of this verb would be used for the latter, but Haupt points to 1 Sam. 24:1 (MT 24:2) for an example of the impersonal usage. 2 Sam. 15:31 might be another example, though it has its own text-critical problems.

traditional reading. Either way, Mordecai is reported to Haman because he is Jewish. Here we see the central problem for Hebrews in the Empire – how does one remain a loyal citizen when some of the state opposes your existence?[18] It is a problem Christians in many parts of the world face today, and for them, like Mordecai, it is not an abstract issue. Mordecai had shown he could work for the state's well-being when he advised of the plot against the king,[19] but he apparently would not honour someone when that meant contradicting God's declared opposition to Amalek, a decision that placed him under threat from those opposed to his people. It is a challenge known to people of faith today who must face the question of how we remain faithful to God's call on our lives with the demands of a state which, even if it guarantees religious freedom, excludes practices shaped by faith within the areas it regulates. This is the problem that runs through the story, and which the book as a whole begins to answer, even if this state's demands were not those of the secular state faced by many in the West today. But before we come to answers it is enough to know the problem's reality.

Amazingly, Haman had seemingly not noticed Mordecai refusing to honour him. But now he sees Mordecai while others prostrate themselves. Like Ahasuerus, Haman has an ego that bruises easily, and the sight of Mordecai not honouring him fills him with anger, taking it as a personal affront even though it is actually the king's command that Mordecai transgresses.[20] Many are angered by others but cannot to do anything about it. But Haman is not like that. He has become the Empire's most senior official, and he can and will act. But he is also prepared to renew an old conflict, and so despises the idea of simply executing Mordecai as he could have done since Mordecai had transgressed the king's command. Rather, elevating the anti-Jewish sentiment hinted at in the officials' report identifying Mordecai, he decided to destroy all the Jews across every province of the Empire. Just as the king could not distinguish between a personal affront and a genuine threat to the Empire when Vashti refused to attend his party,[21] so Haman takes Mordecai's refusal to prostrate himself as reason for attacking all the Jews. But where the king was an alcohol-fuelled fool, Haman is pure malice. This is no longer a conflict between two men. It is an opportunity to reach into the past and settle old scores. Amalek and Israel are old enemies, and Amalek now seems to have the upper hand.

[18] Official Persian policy was ethnically inclusive, but we must here reckon with personal attitudes.
[19] 2:22.
[20] L. M. Day, *Esther* (Nashville: Abingdon, 2005), p. 68.
[21] 1:10–22.

c. Casting the lot (3:7)

We might expect Haman to immediately enact his plan to destroy all Mordecai's people. Yet, instead he arranges for the *Pur* to be cast before him.[22] Mention of the Persian word *pûr*, which is immediately defined as a lot,[23] also provides the rationale for calling the subsequent feast *Purim*, since this is its plural form.[24] Casting lots was associated with finding a propitious date, so it was probably cast by an astrologer. The date chosen is in the last month of the year, meaning that almost an entire year must pass before Haman's plan can unfold. Although many have thought this improbable, one cannot rule out the effects of superstition on people's thinking. Even today, many make important decisions on the basis of horoscopes, and President Reagan was rumoured to have consulted astrologers. In any case, since there is no escape from the Persian Empire it also enables anti-Jewish sentiments to be inflated while increasing Jewish foreboding. Yet it will also provide the means by which their deliverance is achieved. There is thus a hint of one of the 'divine' coincidences that permeate the book. Haman's 'lucky' day actually leaves time to affect deliverance. The question of who controls time is thus implicitly raised, and since the opening chapters have already shown that real power lies with God alone we are prepared for the possibility that overweening human pride and massed power may not be as all pervasive as they seem.

Proverbs 16:33 affirms that Yahweh controls the lot, so Haman's search for a lucky day might actually show that he is under God's control. Yet, the book retains an important tension, because even when it hints that the people of God might know a better outcome it never denies the reality of the pain they experience, for we only know of this possibility retrospectively. There is always the danger that Christians will point to our ultimate victory in Christ, but then ignore the suffering of God's people in many places (both individually and corporately). Esther will not permit this. God's final victory is assured, but God's people also suffer under the oppressor's jackboot. The challenge is to keep both the hope of final victory and the reality of current pain in a proper tension, a tension Paul holds for us in Philippians 1:29, where he reminds us that although we live with the hope of Christ this is a life that is lived in the context of suffering. Here, the emphasis is on the present pain, but with just the hint of something more.

[22] The verb *hippîl* could be understood as indicating Haman cast it himself, but since it was cast before him we have to assume it was done by another.

[23] In this instance, a clay die.

[24] 9:26.

Yet the date that this happened is remarkable. It is the day before Passover.[25] The following day was the time for celebrating God's great moment of salvation in the Old Testament, a time for reflection on how he overcame Pharaoh and his forces. The date gives pause for thought. God had saved his people from a seemingly impossible situation as an enslaved people trapped in a massive Empire. Could he do it again? Scripture never guarantees that God's people will be delivered from every threat, but at least one reason we continue to remember God's saving acts in the past is that remembering them reflectively enables us to face new challenges. For those celebrating that Passover, such questions would take on a real immediacy.

2. Confusion from a decree (3:8–15)

a. A meeting with the king (3:8–11)

Setting a date for the pogrom left Haman with one unresolved problem. How can he issue a decree to destroy the Jews? Even he could not simply wipe out a whole people. Fortunately for Haman, Ahasuerus proved as malleable as ever, and effectively authorised Haman to carry out his plot.

Haman's sense of urgency is apparent from the fact that he approached the king on the same day. He introduces the Jews obliquely, not naming them but gradually building up a case for their destruction by moving from what was undoubtedly true to something that was at best partially true, and finally to a complete falsehood. It is his ability to mix fact and falsehood that makes him dangerous, and of course lies which include a certain amount of truth are always hardest to rebut because one can be taken in by their initial assumptions. Haman begins by observing that they were scattered and dispersed throughout the Empire, a point he emphasises with a neat play on two similar sounding Hebrew words,[26] treating them as an ethnic group, not a religious one. This was undoubtedly true, for although many had returned to Judah at the end of the exile,[27] others remained in Babylon and gradually moved to different provinces. From this he develops a second point, which is that their laws (*dāt*) are different from all the other people. This is, at best, a half truth since *Torah* does not require anyone to disobey

[25] Lev. 23:5.
[26] It is possible that the second also has the sense of 'isolated', so that the Jews are not fully integrated into the life of the empire. So, T. S. Laniak, 'Esther', in L. C. Allen and T. S. Laniak, *Ezra, Nehemiah, Esther* (Peabody: Hendrickson, 2003), p. 218.
[27] Ezra 1 – 2.

state laws, and the differences are primarily religious. Finally, Haman comes to his untruth, which is that the Jews do not obey the king's laws. The form of his statement suggests this is habitual, although the only case that can be pointed out is Mordecai's refusal to bow down. From this comes the grand conclusion – it is not in the king's interests to allow them to remain in his kingdom. Haman sounds like a reasonable civil servant. That he is not free from self interest becomes clear in verse 9 where he effectively offers the king a bribe of ten thousand talents of silver. The sum is incredible,[28] perhaps hyperbolic (after all, everything in Ahasuerus' court is exaggerated), probably over half the Empire's annual tax revenue. How Haman hoped to obtain it is unclear unless he believed it would be seized from those eliminated. It does, however, balance the claim that there was no profit in allowing the Jews to remain since the profit here is indisputable.

The king's response in verses 10–11 is essentially an abdication of responsibility, since handing over the royal signet ring meant Haman was free to issue decrees as if from the king himself, the ring being equivalent to his signature. Remarkably, Ahasuerus does not even ask which people are to be destroyed,[29] while Haman now receives an additional title – *the enemy of the Jews*. Responsible government was clearly not Ahasuerus' strength. A similar transfer occurs in 8:2, though for a better arrangement than this. What is meant by verse 11 is obscure. It could mean that the king declines the bribe, suggesting that it was beneath his dignity to accept it and sully his hands with the matter.[30] However, he could be obliquely accepting it, as if to say – 'You can spend the money how you want'[31] – and thus accepting it. Given Esther's later statement that her people have been sold (7:4), the latter is more probable. We should perhaps note the parallel in Genesis 23:14–15 where Ephron the Hittite seemingly indicates there is no need for Abraham to pay for the field to bury Sarah when in fact the sum mentioned was the amount required. Perhaps more importantly, it provides a horrific example of Edmund Burke's oft cited dictum that 'All that is necessary for the triumph of evil is that good men do nothing.' Perhaps blinded by the size of the bribe offered, Ahasuerus looked

[28] Over three hundred tons.

[29] It is possible that the king thinks Haman has referred only to enslavement, since the verb 'to destroy' sounds almost identical with the verb 'to enslave' (cf. C. M. Bechtel, *Esther* [Louisville: Westminster John Knox, 2002], pp. 42–43, for a summary of the case), but it is difficult to sustain an argument to such an inferential level.

[30] So L. B. Paton, *A Critical and Exegetical Commentary on the Book of Esther* (Edinburgh: T & T Clark, 1908), p. 206.

[31] So Moore, *Esther*, p. 40; D. J. A. Clines, *Ezra, Nehemiah, Esther* (Grand Rapids: Eerdmans, 1984), p. 297.

the other way. By this he connived with evil, setting in train a process with monstrous consequences, just as many since have looked the other way while massive abuses were launched by National Socialism or Idi Amin and their ilk. God's people are called to practise justice,[32] and this story is a constant reminder of why we need vigilance in examining the work of those in power. In Ahasuerus' case, there is also the tragic irony that he has a Jewish wife, and it was a Jew who had saved his life, though they will become the centres of resistance to Haman's plan.

b. A decree issued (3:12–15)

The book's fascination with written texts continues in verse 12, echoing the earlier decree from 1:22. So the day before Passover,[33] the scribes were summoned to issue Haman's dreadful decree. The process describes the immense detail involved in sending out such a decree. Scribes were gathered and the decree was translated into every language and script of the Empire to ensure everybody understood. Similarly, special copies were made for government officials, presumably because they needed reminding of their part in the decree. Although the decree was sealed by the king's signet ring and so came with his authority, all that was written was at Haman's command. The king was complicit, but there is no doubt who was the prime instigator. Special couriers were needed to send out this terrifying decree. In the midst of this, the decree's dreadful contents are summarised. All the Jews were to be destroyed, killed, annihilated, young and old, male and female. None were to be left. It was butchery on a vast scale, with language piled up in gruesome repetition to emphasise the horror, a horror repeated many times in events like the Holocaust or the genocides in Rwanda and Bosnia, but which continues in the experience of people of faith in many parts of the world today. Additionally, the Jews were to be plundered, presumably to pay for Haman's bribe, though this is not stated.

This decree was to be everywhere, a perennial reminder of what was coming and could not be escaped, and an enduring reminder to all others of their duty to the Empire. All had to be ready. Moreover, it is only now that we learn that the thirteenth of Adar is to be the fateful day.

With the decree posted in the city of Susa,[34] Ahasuerus resumed his favourite pastime, and settled down for a drink with Haman.

[32] Amos 5:24; Matt. 23:23.
[33] Babylonians would have regarded the thirteenth as an unlucky day to act, so this again stresses Haman's urgency.
[34] That is, the lower city, outside the acropolis.

Their abuse of power is satirised, because all they do is generate confusion amongst their people, Jew and Gentile alike. This confusion shows why believers need to keep a vigilant eye on those in power. Where chapter 2 showed that it is possible to live and function, even within an oppressive state, this chapter shows that limits remain. The notable thing is that even those who are not the intended victims suffer from it, while the perpetrators find ways of closing themselves off from its implications. Biblical faith will not, however, permit such actions to remain unchallenged, and the allusions to Passover hint at an alternative view, one that (echoing chapter 1), knows that the only power to which we ultimately submit is that of God. The Bible generally encourages believers to submit to the state's authority,[35] but this is never an uncritical acceptance because it also knows that the state sometimes embodies all that is opposed to God.[36] The community's confusion here is a sure sign that this was a time when the state's workings needed both to be scrutinised and resisted.

As we take this chapter seriously, we recognise that its concerns with the abuse of power need to be worked out in two directions. By showing the folly of both the king and Haman and the confusion they bring to all, the chapter implicitly directs us to a different model of leadership. Jesus makes it very clear that our leadership is to be modelled on him, and that must mean servant leadership.[37] Yet it is an undoubted tragedy that the reason behind many church splits is often more to do with power than the doctrinal issues that are claimed. So long as we seek to claim power for ourselves we deny the pattern Jesus has set for us and fall instead into the pattern of Haman and Ahasuerus. Yet it is the distinctiveness of our leadership that is essential to allowing the people of God to grow. Hence, we need to take seriously the warning evident in this chapter and recognise that something very different is required of us. But as we seek to establish an alternative model of leadership with the church we are also enabled to follow the second direction hinted at here. The book of Esther's critique of Haman and Ahasuerus comes from a context where Mordecai will ultimately work for the well-being of all, even if he retained a focus on his own people. Hence, the critique of abusive power comes from a people who appreciate there is another way. As the church follows Jesus' pattern of servant leadership we are then able to offer effective criticism of other patterns of leadership, whether that be political, economic or social. It is the gospel itself which should lead us to make a stand for

[35] Rom. 13:1–7; 1 Pet. 2:2–17.
[36] Rev. 13.
[37] Mark 10:35–45.

justice, whether this happens within our own immediate community or more widely.[38] Christians thus need to be at the forefront of moves to establish justice both locally and globally, even as we continue to trust in the hope of what God will ultimately do.

[38] Mark 10:45; Mic. 6:8.

4:1–17
4. Risking all

Richard Foster has observed that 'superficiality is the curse of our age'.[1] Foster's response to this problem is to encourage the church to rediscover the classical devotional disciplines such as prayer, fasting, and meditation. Other than fasting, though seemingly shorn of its religious connotations, none of Foster's disciplines appears in Esther. Nevertheless, the problem of superficiality does emerge in this chapter as a problem to be overcome as Mordecai has to convince Esther to take a stand for her people. He does so in what is probably the book's best known chapter. Reasons for its relative popularity are not hard to find. In a book that is seemingly so secular, a passage that comes near to a direct theological statement has an evident appeal, even if that statement is not actually made. Indeed, calling a fast without mentioning prayer is remarkable since elsewhere in the Old Testament fasting usually occurs in the context of prayer,[2] though mourning can also feature.[3] Here, just when it seems most likely that God will be mentioned, we meet a gaping theological silence. As Berlin observes, 'God is most present and most absent in this chapter.'[4] Yet the book assumes God's activity, evident in God-shaped holes in the narrative, and these become apparent from a close reading of the text.[5] Somehow, in the faithful

---

[1] R. J. Foster, *Celebration of Discipline: The Path to Spiritual Growth* (San Francisco: Harper Collins, 1988), p. 1.

[2] E.g. Ezra 8:23; Neh. 1:4; Jer. 14:12. It is notable that GNB thus adds prayer in its translation of Esth. 4:16 even though no reference to prayer occurs in either MT or LXX. AT does mention prayer, but it omits the fast.

[3] Zech. 7:5. Both elements are apparent in 2 Sam. 12:16–23.

[4] A. Berlin, *Esther: The Traditional Hebrew Text with the New JPS Translation* (Philadelphia: Jewish Publication Society, 2001), p. 44. See also D. Reid, *Esther: An Introduction and Commentary* (Nottingham: IVP, 2008), p. 106.

[5] J. A. Loader, 'Esther as a Novel with Various Levels of Meaning', *ZAW* 90, pp. 417–421.

action of God's people we discover the working of God for his people.

What can be lost in a search for overtly theological material is the immense skill with which the narrative is constructed. Much of it is a conversation between Esther and Mordecai that is conducted through intermediaries who gradually fade from view as we go deeper into the discussion. Further, the dialogue begins with Mordecai ordering Esther, but ends with Mordecai doing as Esther has ordered him. It reverses the image of the obedient girl who went to the palace, preparing us for how Esther, the 'more suitable girl,' will come to dominate the king. The chapter is a thus crucial for the book's plot. The problem has been established, and Mordecai, although partly responsible, cannot change things himself. But he realises that Esther can, and hints at a possible divine cause in her appointment that will allow her to bring relief and deliverance to her people.

1. Mordecai in mourning (4:1–3)

Having left Mordecai while the decree against the Jews was issued, we now return to him. This is part of a process of scene shifts that run through until chapter 7, when all the central characters are present. Mordecai, we are told, knew what had been done. He not only knew a decree had been issued, but also how it happened, though the extent of his knowledge is only gradually revealed through his dialogue with Esther. Mordecai is thus contrasted with Ahasuerus, who should know but chooses not to. Mordecai does not need to know what has happened, but he does. We are not told how Mordecai knows, and though one can imagine gossip among the courtiers the narrator is not interested in such detail. The point is rather that God's people know what is happening in their world because such knowledge is itself the basis for action. For Mordecai, this knowledge will be his evidence in convincing Esther to take a radical stand for her people. A proper knowledge of current events (rather than something partially formed from some headlines) is equally vital for Christians today if we are to address pressing issues in our society so that our work is properly directed to those places where the gospel can significantly address social concerns.

Mordecai's mourning is typical of the region. Tearing clothes and the putting on sackcloth (possibly goat or camel hair) and ashes are mentioned several times in the Old Testament,[6] usually stressing the pain of those who mourn. Anderson notes a possible vestige of earlier

---

[6] E.g. 2 Kgs 18:37.

religious practices,[7] especially since ashes are associated with the purificatory ritual of the red heifer,[8] though formalised behaviour is not always conscious of drawing on earlier patterns. Something similar can be said of Mordecai's great and mournful cry, which would typically represent a lament rooted in a relationship with God.[9] Certainly a cry of 'violence' would fit here[10] though if Mordecai knows he triggered this horror then he would have good reason to cry out about what he has done! Yet even if the crisis was triggered by Mordecai's refusal to offer homage to Haman,[11] the narrative never blames him for what has happened since to do so would blame the victim for the crime.[12] Such an attitude can develop all too easily, but the book of Esther is conscious that, although our actions have consequences, we cannot control how others will react to us. But Mordecai did not mourn alone; he was joined by all the Jews throughout the Empire who also fasted, wept and wailed.[13] All of this was classically meant to draw God's attention to what is happening though it could not compel him to act.[14] Yet the narrator refrains from making any overt religious comment because although we see behaviour that typically marked serious prayer, the emphasis here is on the faithful response of God's people to the crisis. The book of Esther does not deny the value of prayer. Instead, it stresses that the people of God frequently have both to trust God and to take seriously their own role in putting right the things about which they pray.

In the midst of this Mordecai came to the entrance of the palace gate but could go no further because those dressed for mourning could not enter. No reason is given for this prohibition which may simply be court etiquette.[15] His mourning, and that of his people, is evident for all to see, so by standing at the entrance to the gate he does enough to make sure he is noticed but not enough to create

---

[7] B. Anderson, 'The Book of Esther' in G. W. Buttrick (ed), *The Interpreter's Bible* vol. 3 (Nashville: Abingdon, 1954), p. 852.

[8] Num. 19:9–10.

[9] R. N. Boyce, *The Cry to God in the Old Testament* (Atlanta: Scholar's Press, 1988), p. 1.

[10] D. J. A. Clines, *Ezra, Nehemiah, Esther* (Grand Rapids: Eerdmans, 1984), p. 299.

[11] So, S. W. Crawford, 'Esther', in L. E. Keck (ed.), *The New Interpreter's Bible*, vol. 3 (Nashville: Abingdon, 1999), p. 902.

[12] M. V. Fox, *Character and Ideology in the Book of Esther* (2nd ed., Grand Rapids: Eerdmans, 2001), p. 57.

[13] Cf. Joel 2:12. K. H. Jobes, in *Esther: The NIV Application Commentary* (Grand Rapids: Zondervan, 1999), pp. 135–137, thinks there may be a deliberate intertextual echo here, helping create the theological background for this chapter.

[14] Cf. Isa. 58:3.

[15] Clines, *Ezra, Nehemiah, Esther*, p. 299, points to Herodotus 3:119 as a possible parallel, though it is not necessarily the case that the peasants crying out for water at the gate there are following this particular rule.

further trouble for himself. Mordecai has stood in a similar place before and been able to communicate with Esther[16] and apparently came to do so again. God knows the need of his people, and Mordecai knows that this crisis is not a time for sitting and waiting. It is a time for faithful (but not foolhardy) action to discover where God will act. It is taking the risk of faith in order to summon others to do the same.

2. Esther's first response (4:4–9)

Although all the Jews were mourning because of the king's decree, Mordecai's actions were conspicuous enough to come to Esther's attention via her maids and eunuchs. There was, presumably, a useful grapevine amongst palace staff, and in spite of the evident difficulties it is clear that Mordecai and Esther were able to communicate through the staff. Here, it seems that the palace staff have taken the initiative to report what had happened, suggesting that they were well aware of the relationship between Esther and Mordecai. Esther's response is not entirely clear because the word used here occurs nowhere else. Most translations suggest she 'writhed' greatly, though Moore notes that the LXX would suggest she was 'perplexed.'[17] However, LXX may have mistaken two similar Hebrew roots, and perhaps we have an idiomatic way of saying Esther was greatly shocked.[18] But shocked at what? At this point we do not know if it is the decree or Mordecai's behaviour, though sending Mordecai clothing would suggest that his behaviour was the problem, and it is only through the ensuing dialogue that we discover that Esther was ignorant of the decree. Mordecai, however, refuses to accept her gift, drawing her on to find out why he was mourning so publicly. In effect, although Esther herself will show that she is not superficial, she still looks for the superficial response. Like many who confront major problems, her first response is to seek the solution that involves the lowest level of commitment. Thus, Mordecai is inappropriately dressed for the palace gate, so she sends him clothing to address this problem. But Mordecai brusquely refused to accept it. As a result, Esther is forced to inquire why he was behaving so unusually, something that she commands Hathak, one of the eunuchs appointed for her by the king, to discover from Mordecai. Complex problems are seldom solved by a quick and easy answer (however appealing it might seem), and Mordecai will not let Esther avoid the problem here with a simple answer.

[16] 2:11, 22.
[17] C. A. Moore, *Esther* (Garden City: Doubleday, 1971), p. 48.
[18] P. Haupt, 'Critical Notes on Esther', *AJSL* 24 (1907–8), p. 134.

The conversation between Mordecai and Esther takes place through Hathak, although he gradually fades from the narrative. Mordecai's answer to Esther is remarkably detailed. He reports the exact amount of money that Haman had promised to pay into the royal treasuries for their extermination, also providing a copy of the decree authorising it, issued in Susa. This was to be shown and explained to Esther, perhaps suggesting that she was unable to read, though it may simply be that Hathak was to explain the exact situation to her. Mordecai understands that evidence is important because the sort of decision he will ask Esther to make cannot simply be on the basis of assertions. Esther must thus know that this is not a personal problem for Mordecai for which a quick fix would suffice. Instead, it was a crisis engulfing all her people throughout the Empire. In doing this, Mordecai prepared for his request to Esther – that she should go to the king and seek grace for her people. Doing this *on behalf of her people* meant revealing her own ethnic identity,[19] even though Mordecai's awareness of anti-Jewish sentiment had previously meant she was to keep this to herself. Esther could function within the Empire without revealing her people provided it did not threaten them, but where the Empire threatens her people it was essential that she declare her identity. In a conflict between the state and her faith and people, identifying with her faith and people must take priority. All this Hathak duly reports, leaving Esther with an awkward challenge.

Esther's obedience to her guardian is being challenged in a most awkward manner since obedience here involves risks not previously present. Indeed, although Mordecai is not Esther's actual parent he acts in that role for her, so this dialogue also explores something of what the fifth commandment might mean. Honouring parents for Esther will also mean taking a risk for the security of her people precisely because the one who has acted in place of her parents has asked her to do so. Mordecai has presented the information and there are no longer any easy answers.

3. Breaking through to commitment (4:10–17)

a. Persuading Esther (4:10–14)

Against Mordecai's suggestion, Esther has a ready made excuse that Hathak duly reports. What's more, Esther implies that this is something Mordecai should know since everyone else in the Empire

---

[19] F. B. Huey, 'Esther', in Frank E. Gaebelein (ed.), *The Expositor's Bible Commentary*, vol. 4 (Grand Rapids: Zondervan, 1988), p. 817.

does. Put simply, it is against the law for her to go to the king without having been first summoned.[20] And to make sure Mordecai realises the seriousness of this she adds the point that for anyone entering the inner courtyard without having been summoned then there was only one law – that they be put to death. It didn't matter who it was who entered without the summons, the outcome was the same. Yet even as Esther speaks, she introduces our first exception clause in Persian law – if the king wishes, he can extend his sceptre and grant that the person may live. Although there are no clear parallels to this statement from other sources on the Persians it is not difficult to imagine the existence of such a law. Autocrats usually have no time for others, and there was a normal process of making appointments to see the king. Indeed, it is a functionally necessary element for those in power that they are shielded from the possibility of anyone coming to see them as and when they want. But lest Mordecai think that this exception provides Esther with some hope she then points out that it is some thirty days since she was summoned to see the king. Although this may sound odd to us, it is not unlikely where a king has several wives, and in any case since the king's choice of Esther was a fundamentally a lust match[21] it is entirely probable. Esther's response is that Mordecai's request is simply impossible because the king's ardour has cooled to such an extent that the exception clause would not operate. The law was meant to stop lawless intruders reaching the king, not to prevent the queen seeing him.[22] But with a level of inflexibility that is typical of Persian law it has also caught out an innocent wife. Esther now knows that a simple response is insufficient, but she cannot see that there is anything she can do. She thus stands between the superficial response and the committed one, but without an obvious option to enable her to make the committed response. As still happens to many today, she can see a complex problem, but cannot see a way through it.

Mordecai's response is blunt and to the point. Esther should not imagine she will be the only Jew to survive because she is separated from them by living in the palace. She will die whether she goes to see the king or not. He concludes in verse 14 with what is perhaps the most famous verse in the book, though its interpretation is disputed. That Esther cannot remain silent and that Mordecai anticipates deliverance from somewhere is clear enough, but the balance of the verse is ambiguous, perhaps intentionally so. What

[20] See also Herodotus, *History*, 3.140.
[21] 2:14.
[22] J. G. Baldwin, *Esther: An Introduction and Commentary* (Leicester: IVP, 1984), p. 79.

does he mean by *another place*? Although later Rabbinic writings use 'place' (*māqôm*) as a euphemism for the name of God such usage offers little help here since this is '*another* place'. However, this usage cannot disprove a reference to God here[23] since it probably derives (in part) from this passage.[24] Nevertheless, '*another place*' could refer to political deliverance, so Mordecai might simply mean somewhere else, like Greece. His veiled reference to providence might also suggest a reference to God, though of course God could act through another nation. As always in the book of Esther, the theological reference is veiled. Of course, the way the book expresses its theology does not mean that the political and theological interpretations are mutually exclusive.[25] Similarly, Mordecai's comment on the fate of Esther's family might point to the threat of divine punishment if Esther does not respond, though it might simply assert that even in the palace it will be impossible for Esther to escape. But Mordecai is confident that deliverance will come, whether or not it is through Esther, and that confidence is meant to make readers ponder the possibility of God's involvement without indicating exactly how it might come about.

The final clause of verse 14 takes the argument one step further. The question, *And who knows*, leaves it open for Esther to consider. She has become queen at just the right time. His question thus asks Esther to ponder providence. Is it possible that she has been placed in this position just so she can serve God's purposes? It is precisely because we cannot know such things in advance that the question is phrased as it is, but it is a question that many since Esther have also had to consider. Joseph understood that what his brothers had meant for evil God meant for good,[26] and that he had been placed in an unexpected position of authority to fulfil God's purposes for his people. But Joseph could look back and know this. Esther here, however, is like most of us when confronted by a challenge, especially if we confront some form of evil (even if not as heinous as that she faced). Mordecai's question has no easy answer, but it suggests that often enough God has prepared in advance for the challenges his people will face and that we are therefore called to recognise this and challenge evil when we see it. In the New

[23] Contra Clines, *Ezra, Nehemiah, Esther*, p. 302, with T. S. Laniak, 'Esther', in L. C. Allen and T. S. Laniak, *Ezra, Nehemiah, Esther* (Peabody: Hendrickson, 2003), p. 227.

[24] F. Bush, *Ruth/Esther* (Dallas: Word, 1996), p. 396, though he interprets the sentence as insisting that deliverance will not arise apart from Esther, taking it as a rhetorical question with an expected negative answer. Although questions in Hebrew can be unmarked, greater contextual evidence is required to accept this interpretation.

[25] B. W. Anderson, 'The Book of Esther', p. 854.

[26] Gen. 45:5–7; 50:18–21.

Testament, James would call this the point where faith and works come together,[27] and there is no doubt that we are called to challenge evil when we see it.

b. Esther takes control (4:15–17)

A decisive shift in Esther's approach now takes place. Where previously she has been passive, a Jew who the king presumes to be a pagan, someone known only for her beauty and submission to men around her, now she moves to control her own circumstances. The element of Mordecai's argument that convinced her is not stated, though it would be hard to resist his moral arm twisting.[28] It is now Esther who orders Mordecai and not Mordecai who orders Esther. Esther takes control from here and continues to do so until she introduces the king to Mordecai in chapter 8, from which point Mordecai is more prominent. Esther's directions to Mordecai are simple and direct. The imperative 'go' that begins verse 16 is explained by second sentence. Mordecai is to gather all the Jews on the administrative acropolis (since they would be accessible to him), and fast for three days. The fast's conditions are severe, with no eating or drinking for three days, a clear contrast to the regular feasting and drinking of the king and Haman.[29] It is a demanding fast for the Jews, though one that would be shared by Esther and her maidens (who are presumably not Jewish). Moreover, if these events are on the day the decree was issued then it means fasting over Passover, the very time when Jews were meant to feast and celebrate their deliverance from Egypt. There is no more space for a simple solution. A demanding and complex challenge requires absolute commitment to God and his people, including the possibility of putting aside what might be considered the normal practice of faith. Just as Aaron declined to eat the sacrifices following the death of his sons, even though this was expected, so Esther may have to miss Passover because of a pressing evil.[30]

This fast is clearly different from the one mentioned in verse 3 which was related more to mourning. The new fast is to prepare Esther for her entry to see the king, highlighting incidentally that fasting may be done for a number of different reasons. Exactly how this would be achieved is not stated, although the common association of fasting with prayer suggests that this is a summons to divine

[27] Jas 2:14–26.
[28] It is not impossible that Paul's arguments concerning Onesimus to Philemon are, at least indirectly, influenced by Mordecai's approach.
[29] 1:1–9; 2:18; 3:15.
[30] Lev. 10:16–20.

aid. But in keeping with the rest of the book, this is only implied because the emphasis is upon the faithfulness of God's servants. Here, it is as Esther and her people commit themselves to God that they also commit themselves to each other. A phrase that is often enough heard among Christians is to 'let go and let God'. If we understand this to mean that there are things we cannot achieve ourselves, then it is in line with Scripture. But it can also be a cop out which assumes that we have no meaningful role to play in bringing about real change in our world. Esther's fast challenges this sort of thinking. We commit ourselves absolutely to the work and purposes of God in our world, trusting that God will work, but also striving with every fibre of our being to see them brought about. Paul understood this in his work for the gospel,[31] but Esther shows that the principle has a wider applicability within the mission of God.

Prepared by the fast, Esther will go to the king, even though this is against the law. It is a supremely dangerous moment for her in that she must risk the king's ire. Nevertheless, she is prepared to go, and if she dies in the attempt, then she is prepared for that. It is not a simple expression of fatalism that says that whatever will be will be.[32] Rather, the famous words, *if I perish, I perish*, are an expression of courage uttered by one who has placed her life in the hands of providence but who still knows that martyrdom for her people may be the outcome.[33] Ironically, Vashti was excluded because she did not come to the king,[34] but for Esther the risk is going to him. It is important to note that at this point Esther has no idea whether her plan will succeed or not, because we cannot compel God to work with us to achieve goals we set. But we do know that God works to achieve his purposes and calls us to join him in this. It is the ambiguity of this world that Esther explores, and is perhaps one of the key reasons why God is not mentioned directly. We only recognise the working of providence by looking back, but we have to commit ourselves to God's providence and live our lives going forward. Where the Joseph story or the narratives of Daniel and his friends can look back and see how God has worked, the book of Esther shields us from this knowledge. It confronts us, rather, with the important reality that, while there is no room for superficiality, we cannot know in advance what our commitment will cost us. At the same time, Esther also demonstrates that commitment is not

[31] Col. 1:29.
[32] L. B. Paton, *A Critical and Exegetical Commentary on the Book of Esther* (Edinburgh: T & T Clark, 1908), p. 226.
[33] L. M. Day, *Esther* (Nashville: Abingdon, 2005), p. 86.
[34] 1:10–22.

equated with taking foolhardy risks, because she does prepare before she goes to the king. Importantly, we also see that this commitment is shared as, in a neat reversal of roles, Mordecai goes and does all that Esther had commanded him to do. Genuine commitment always works in multiple directions as it invites others to join us in it.

Esther, in committing herself to her people is thus risking all for the faith of her people. It is important to stress, however, that this is not a foolhardy act, and neither is it one in which Esther acts out of ignorance. Her commitment can come precisely because she is well informed about the need of her people and is beginning to see that God has placed her where she is for a purpose, even though God's purposes are not limited to her alone. That is, her commitment is a response to a need that has been laid before her. I would want to distinguish this from what is sometimes presented as taking a risk for faith. I have on several occasions had someone suggest to me that they were considering giving up something significant because this would demonstrate their faith since they would then be dependent upon God to provide a replacement. Each time I have counselled them (not always successfully) against such a choice because in none of these cases was there any evidence that God was calling them to act in this way. Giving up a job so God can replace it with another of the same type is not risking all for faith. Rather, it reverses the process so that we effectively demand God act to prove our faith rather than our faithful actions being a response to what God is doing, following the opportunities that God has placed before us. That is why we must appreciate the fact that Esther responds to the evidence that Mordecai presents to her. Risking all for faith is an informed decision that is superficial in neither its understanding of faith nor of the context in which we find ourselves. Jesus counsels us to consider the cost of discipleship,[35] so we must understand that following him is always costly, but its cost is precisely in the area of discipleship and it is here that Jesus expects us to act on the basis of information. We cannot make any risk we choose to take an act of faith, but where God has laid open the challenge to us then we are called to consider the cost, and then to make the informed decision to follow where he has led.

[35] Luke 14:25–33.

5:1–14
5. A tale of two banquets

Mordecai's challenge to Esther and her subsequent response have been a necessary element in the plan to thwart Haman's intentions. However, the fact of Esther's commitment to her people has provided no specific assurance that she will succeed in her aim – or even if she will be able to see the king without being executed for her actions. Chapter 4 has thus ended with some important unresolved tensions. It is the purpose of chapter 5 to go one step further and begin to show how Haman's plans are going to unravel. Nevertheless, it is important to realise that we are entering into a world of ambiguity. It is not that the text itself is ambiguous (though it carefully leaves key points unresolved), but rather that it brings us into a world where right commitments do not of themselves guarantee good outcomes for all involved. Decisions have to be made without any assurance that they will provide the outcome each individual wants. God does work all things together for the good of his people who are called according to his purpose[1] but that does not mean we each always receive what we want. There is no theological calculus at work that guarantees us freedom from pain and loss even when we are committed to God's people and purposes. Faithfulness, not individual outcomes, is what matters.

Although the chapter contains two distinct scenes, it is apparent that it has a certain unity since it makes a contrast between Esther's wisdom and Haman's folly; the two are clearly contrasted here. Esther acts as Israel's wisdom literature had suggested she should,[2] whilst Haman is portrayed as the archetypal fool, fitting almost precisely the ways in which the fool is described in the book of

---

[1] Rom. 8:28, though it should be noted that this verse has many issues in its own interpretation.
[2] Especially Prov. 13:15; 16:22; 19:11.

Proverbs.[3] Themes of wisdom are thus accented though without reducing Esther or Haman to caricatures. Rather, their story is told in a way that shows the nature of wisdom and folly.

Having committed herself to her people Esther must thus follow through and go to the king. It is important to note that even though in doing so she clearly makes careful preparation she still cannot control the outcomes. Esther's wisdom lies in the fact that she integrates commitment to God's purposes for his people with careful craft in dealing with the king. Yet by the end of this chapter we don't know how this will resolve itself since the king's promise to come to a further banquet appears to give Esther the result she desires, and yet Haman's encounter with Mordecai suggests that Esther will lose her guardian before anything else is resolved. Esther thus lives in a world where God's activity cannot always be predicted but where faithfulness is still paramount.

1. Esther's first audience (5:1–8)

Although the whole of this section relates to Esther's first audience with the king, there are two scenes within it. In the opening (verses 1–4) the location is the inner court of the palace, whilst verses 5–8 are at Esther's banquet. However, verse 5 acts as a seam that indicates that we are to read the events of the two locations together. What is remarkable is that in both locations Ahasuerus seemingly offers Esther the very opportunity that she seeks, even if it is couched in the hyperbole of the royal court. Esther, however, will refuse to make the full request clear either time. Although this is frequently interpreted purely as an example of literary retardation, deferring the main plot to heighten the suspense,[4] she could have another purpose in mind, especially when we remember the narrator's strategy of restricting our knowledge of the motives of the characters. Of course, the deferral *does* heighten the suspense, but that may be part of the game Esther must play if she is to succeed.

The time signal in verse 1 immediately points back to the previous chapter's three-day fast. That has now ended and Esther must prepare herself to meet the king without knowing what will happen, something she does with skill and care. Where Mordecai had come as close to the king as was possible for someone mourning in 4:1–3, Esther comes as close as possible for one who is properly attired.

[3] Especially Prov. 12:16; 13:16, 20; 14:8; 15:14; 17:16; 20:3; 26:7–9; 27:3; 29:9, 11. Proverbs uses different terms for 'fool' in these passages, but their semantic range overlaps.

[4] So C. A. Moore, *Esther* (Garden City: Doubleday, 1971), pp. 57ff.

The care with which she did so is apparent from the statement that she 'put on royalty'.[5] This certainly refers to her royal robes, though the slightly ambiguous terminology may also highlight the lengths to which she had gone.[6] Where she previously wore only what Hegai suggested,[7] now Esther takes the initiative. But given the king's obvious preference for that which is good looking, it was clearly a sensible move to look as attractive as possible. The word 'royal' appears three times in the verse, showing that Esther's choice of clothing was contextually appropriate. The irony is that Esther was, along with her people, actually in mourning, but since sackcloth was not permitted in the king's presence she had to disguise herself in the beauty of royalty. But Esther can only stand in front of the king's throne room since she may not enter without the king's permission. The whole flow of events portrays Esther as a wise woman who is adequately prepared for the challenges of what is to come. Clearly, there is no contradiction between the preparation involved in the fast, and thinking through what is involved in approaching the king. Put another way, times in prayer and fasting do not justify believers in behaving in ways that will alienate those we meet. Spiritual preparation and sensitivity must complement one another, and that is certainly the approach Esther takes here.

The exact nature of the palace rooms described here is unclear as there would appear to be two separate places mentioned (the palace and the hall), but both are referred to simply as 'the king's house' (*bêt hammelek*). However, it may be that because both refer to the one general area that the same term is used.[8] That Esther's planning to this point is successful is immediately apparent. As soon as the king saw her he extended the golden sceptre to her, though until then she stood on that liminal point between success and disaster. The expression *she won favour* is consciously reminiscent of Esther's elevation to the throne in 2:17. Indeed, there are marked parallels between the time of Esther's elevation and her appearance before the king, suggesting in advance that Esther's purposes may be fulfilled, and hinting once again at God's involvement. Both involved a period of preparation and the wearing of special clothes and both lead to Esther gaining favour with the king, though this time it is something Esther actively sought. But the decisive

---

[5] My translation – ESV 'royal robes'.

[6] The addition in LXX here offers a much more dramatic interpretation of Esther's nerves and their effects here.

[7] 2:15.

[8] See J. G. Baldwin, *Esther: An Introduction and Commentary* (Leicester: IVP, 1984), p. 85, for the archaeological details. ESV distinguishes between the 'throne room' and the 'king's quarters'.

difference lies in *why* Esther is present. When taken along with the other beautiful virgins in the Empire she had no choice. She was simply an individual caught up in the machinations of the Empire. But here she comes to the king, at great risk to herself, because she has committed herself to her people. Nevertheless, gaining sufficient favour to approach the king is merely a starting point, so Esther must continue to be an obedient queen, something she demonstrates as she approaches the king and kisses the tip of his sceptre. As Proverbs knows all too well, approaching autocrats must be done with care![9] Gaining an entrance is not enough, and wisdom continues to be necessary to consider what is done next. Likewise, Christians today must not make the mistake of assuming that just because an opportunity is presented for the Gospel that we can blunder in without adequately considering the context in which we find ourselves. Cultural sensitivity is always needed.

A first reading of verse 3 might presume that the king offers Esther everything she seeks, offering up to *half of my kingdom*.[10] But this is essentially a formality that is not meant to be taken seriously.[11] Kings do not, after all, easily give up half of their kingdom. Nevertheless, the king's comments in verse 3 provide Esther with a point of entry from which to develop her position. As is typical of the king, his question comes twice, though the second of these (*What is your request?*) does require some specific information from Esther as opposed to the more general initial inquiry. However unknowing the king may be elsewhere, he knows Esther must have some special reason for taking the risk of standing before him uninvited. With what seems like an open invitation we expect Esther immediately to raise the issue of Haman's decree. What is initially surprising is that she does not. Here we enter one of the points of ambiguity the narrative creates for us. Although plenty have speculated on Esther's motivation for not immediately revealing the actual issue, the narrator refuses to offer us any insight on this point. The effect of this is to let us see only what the king sees – his beautiful (though seemingly somewhat ignored of late) wife has taken the risk of standing before him. Surely, the need must be pressing. But wisdom is not only knowing how to present oneself; it is also a matter of knowing when and how to speak. Good impressions cannot simply be based on appearances. More than

[9] Prov. 14:35; 16:12–15; 19:12; 20:2; 22:11; 23:1–3; 25:3–7.

[10] Herodotus, 9:109–11 records a similar offer. In a conscious echo of this story, Mark 6:22–23 records Herod making a similar offer to Herodias. There, too, a king is shown to be foolish in his dealings with women.

[11] L. B. Paton, *A Critical and Exegetical Commentary on the Book of Esther* (Edinburgh: T & T Clark, 1908), p. 233.

that, wisdom involves having some idea of how things need to be done, even if flexibility is still needed. Esther has found favour with the king before but subsequently found that the king's passions cooled. She cannot, therefore, accept an offer based on appearances alone but rather requires something that can address the appalling position of her people. Wisdom demands a substantial offer, not polite words that cannot be taken seriously.

Esther's response to the king employs the typical language of the court that is so common in chapters 1–2, highlighting the importance of a suggestion pleasing the king, though of course so far *every* suggestion seems good to the king. Such language heightens the expectation that an important request is about to be initiated. But we are in for a surprise because she instead invites both the king and Haman to another banquet that she has prepared.[12] Again, there is a contrast between appearance and experience. Esther has fasted for three days at the end of that period; presumably when she was at her hungriest, she has prepared a banquet. Not mentioning Haman's edict serves to defer the story's denouement, but throughout this encounter there is more going on than meets the eye. A dinner invitation might suggest to the king that Esther is simply seeking more time with him, though the inclusion of Haman also hints at wider concerns. But in light of the delicate situation, a discussion around the dinner table is perhaps more suitable since then Esther will not have to raise the issue of the edict publicly. Indeed, much of Scripture affirms the importance of table fellowship, and Jesus also took the opportunity provided by meals to raise and discuss difficult issues,[13] so choosing a private meal as the occasion to raise her concerns with the king is perhaps not as surprising as many think. Rather, it is a matter of developing a congenial atmosphere where important matters can be discussed without the pressure of more formal structures. Yet even when we note this we must still accept that Esther's motives are never outlined directly, and however much we may think that we can explain them we are kept in the same position as the king and Haman and so do not know exactly what Esther intends. What is clear is that with the banquet prepared she expects the king to come immediately. That the king, not Haman, is the central figure in the dinner is signalled by her use of the masculine singular throughout. Although its detail is only revealed to us gradually, it is clear that Esther has a well thought-out strategy,

[12] S. W. Crawford ('Esther', in L. E. Keck [ed.], *The New Interpreter's Bible*, vol. 3 [Nashville: Abingdon, 1999], p. 908) notes that is culturally inappropriate to make a major request right away. If so, this again shows the importance of cultural awareness in dealing with others.

[13] E.g. Luke 7:36–50; 19:1–10.

and her language is carefully deployed to ensure this strategy has the best possible chance of being achieved.

The value in understanding those with whom you deal is immediately apparent as the king commands that Haman be hurried to the feast. What is worth noting in verse 5 is that the king acts for the first time at the word of Esther – something he will gradually do in more significant ways as the narrative progresses. Thus, the king and Haman come to the banquet. Curiously, where Vashti was deposed for refusing to come to the king's banquet, Esther's stock with the king rises when she invites him to hers. At the banquet, the king again questions Esther, recognising that there is more involved than a simple desire to have dinner. Again, the question comes in two parts and follows the standard pattern of politeness in offering Esther up to half the kingdom. But there is a slight change from verse 3. There, he initially asked about her welfare, with the second question perhaps continuing on that line even though it asked what she sought. Here, both times he focuses on what it is that Esther desires, wanting to know her *wish* and *request*. That this happens while drinking wine indicates that this is the period after the main meal,[14] so Esther has not rushed. As with her appearance before the king, it was vital that once she had created the context, he provide the means for her to take matters further. However pressing Esther's desire might be to address the problem of Haman's decree she understands the importance of waiting for the right opportunity. Nevertheless, although Ahasuerus has offered Esther up to half the kingdom, he cannot expect this to be taken literally.

Esther's answer also comes in two parts. Most modern translations imply a verb at the end of verse 7,[15] but Esther simply repeats the king's words back to him, almost like she is chewing over his words before she begins her answer proper. It is in verse 8 that she then begins to answer the king's request directly. Surprisingly, she again does not take up the issue of Haman's edict, instead inviting the king and Haman to a second banquet. Such brinkmanship has been considered by many as evidence of the fictional nature of the story.[16] But the delay implicit in her answer is not only necessary for the story's structure (although it does heighten the tension). Rather, Esther's carefully worded response suggests that a second banquet was always intended. Her answer in verse 8 is structured around two 'if' clauses, each of which gradually narrows

---

[14] Paton, *A Critical and Exegetical Commentary on the Book of Esther*, p. 236.

[15] E.g. NIV reads, 'My petition and my request is this', thus making verse 8 develop this as an initial statement. But this reading is contrary to the Hebrew and loses the sense of surprise when Esther does reveal her request in the second half of verse 8.

[16] E.g. Moore, *Esther*, p. 58.

the king's range of options. We know that Esther has found favour with the king, and that the king always acts according to advice that he has received. Therefore, Esther's answer is more than simply court formalities, even though she again carefully repeats the king's key terms. As the Hebrew is worded, Esther suggests that the king's very presence at this banquet will be sufficient to oblige him to grant Esther's request.[17] If the king comes to this additional banquet, and he has no excuse *not* to come, then he must give Esther what she wants. Yet only then will Esther actually reveal her request, and all of this is in accordance with the word of the king anyway.[18] Haman had arranged for the Jews' destruction without fully informing the king,[19] so also Esther prepares for their deliverance without revealing her full plan. Here then we see most clearly Esther's wisdom as she seems almost to embody Proverbs' advice on prudent speech.[20] Neither the justice of a cause nor extended time in spiritual preparation can excuse hasty and poorly thought-through speech, since speech is the primary means by which we communicate. The delay of waiting for the next banquet may well increase the narrative tension, but it also means Esther has a guaranteed response once she puts her request to the king.

2. Haman's folly (5:9–14)

Where Esther embodies wisdom, Haman comes across as the classical fool, though he does not know the danger he faces at this point. That he is unaware of his danger is immediately apparent. Haman rejoices that he was at the banquet with the king and queen, and is glad and merry of heart. The last time that anyone's heart was merry was the king in 1:10, just before he made a serious misjudgement concerning Vashti, hinting already that too much alcohol might lead him to a similarly poor decision.[21] Haman is shortly to do this with respect to Mordecai, although at this point his folly will be less apparent. His presenting problem is that Mordecai continues to show him no respect, neither rising nor trembling in Haman's presence. Just as he was in 3:5, Haman was filled with wrath. But this time he controls himself and returns home, where he sends for his friends, whom 6:13 somewhat satirically refers to as his wise

---

[17] Similarly, F. Bush, *Ruth/Esther* (Dallas: Word, 1996), p. 407; D. J. A. Clines, *The Esther Scroll: The Story of the Story* (Sheffield: JSOT Press, 1984), p. 37.

[18] Cf. D. J. A. Clines, *Ezra, Nehemiah, Esther* (Grand Rapids: Eerdmans, 1984), p. 305.

[19] 3:8.

[20] Prov. 15:28; 17:27.

[21] Cf. Judg. 16:25.

men, and his wife Zeresh. We are not told why Esther acted as she did, and Haman's motives are not revealed either. Yet just as Esther's wisdom is progressively revealed through her speech and actions, so also Haman's folly is gradually demonstrated through dialogue. Ultimately, he is concerned to resolve the problem of Mordecai but before doing so he apparently felt the need to boast of the glory of his wealth and the number of his sons. Presumably his wife and friends know this already, just as they know the story of how the king had elevated him above all the other potential officials (presumably including them) to the most important position in the Empire. Certainly his wife would know how many sons he has! Haman is like the fool in Proverbs 13:16; his words reveal his folly. Yet there is a deeper irony here, for Haman will lose each of the things about which he boasts. And the starting point of this loss will occur when Mordecai takes his position in 8:2. The man who plotted to destroy all the Jews will lose everything to them, though at this point it seems as if he is close to his ultimate triumph. His boasting is like someone with an inferiority complex who needs his ego stroked. Such boasting is again consistent with Proverbs' picture of the fool.[22] It is a black comedy, as we see someone completely out of touch with reality, but also realise the dangers such people pose.

The only new information is that Haman alone attended Esther's banquet with the king and has been invited to join the king at Queen Esther's banquet on the next day, though the unusual way he words this points to his self-centredness.[23] This should cement his position but that it is not enough is immediately apparent from verse 13. Mordecai's continued presence in the gate (the participles suggest habitual activity) means Haman has no satisfaction. The offence of Mordecai being in the gate and not offering homage offsets everything else. Haman also makes clear that Mordecai is Jewish, though his wife will later claim surprise about this (6:13). Essentially, we now have the reason given for the gathering – Haman wants advice on what to do with Mordecai, and his Jewishness remains central to the problem. The basic issue is that Haman wants to enjoy the banquet but cannot do so if Mordecai remains because although he gains honour by attending the banquet, Mordecai undermines this through his refusal to offer homage.

The answer is essentially that of Zeresh (the verb is feminine singular) though Haman's friends are apparently in full agreement. Zeresh's answer again demonstrates how dangerous absolute power

---

[22] Cf. Prov. 16:18, 25 and J. G. McConville, *Ezra, Nehemiah, Esther*, (Edinburgh: St Andrew's Press, 1985), p. 177.

[23] L. M. Day, *Esther* (Nashville: Abingdon, 2005), p. 106.

can be. The suggestion is that a stake of some fifty cubits be erected (roughly seventy-five feet, or as high as a cricket pitch is long) on which Mordecai is to be impaled[24] once Haman has spoken to the king. Although the height is probably hyperbolic, it would certainly be high enough to publicly humiliate Mordecai. No crime deserving capital punishment is mentioned, nor is any plausible. Haman is simply to use his authority to destroy Mordecai before the pogrom. What is grotesque in Zeresh's suggestion is that Mordecai's death will enable Haman to enjoy Esther's second banquet, though it will actually provide more scope for poetic justice than anything else.[25] Curiously, where the edict of 1:20–22 had been intended to ensure that wives did as their husbands required, this chapter now has both the king and Haman follow their wives' suggestions, again showing the foolishness of their claims to power. Since Haman is just as capable of acting on foolish advice as the king, he agrees to the proposal.

A darker problem now emerges. Esther has shown great wisdom and tact so that on the next day she will in some way bring about deliverance for all the Jews, though exactly how this will be resolved is not yet clear. But Haman's anger against Mordecai has now put in train a process that will see him executed before Esther can bring this about. Deliverance without Mordecai will, for Esther at least, be a hollow victory. Does this therefore mean that Haman's folly outweighs wisdom?[26] Here, then, we see the world of ambiguity that the narrative creates for us, one in which God's people must indeed commit themselves absolutely to God and yet also use all the wisdom available to them. But these do not of themselves guarantee the outcomes we desire, and wisdom can be undone by folly, especially in a world where there are inequalities in power. We are thus left at this point on an unresolved tension. Both Esther and Haman can sleep well because they believe they have put in place plans that will see their desired outcomes,[27] but Esther also needs God to be at work because she does not know of Haman's plan. Believers may (and indeed must) work with all they have, but we still need the mystery of God's involvement with his people if justice is to be wrought. It is vital, therefore, that we maintain the balance that this chapter retains. Believers are to use every piece of

---

[24] Cf. 2:23.
[25] K. H. Jobes, in *Esther: The NIV Application Commentary* (Grand Rapids: Zondervan, 1999), p. 145, notes parallels with Jezebel's advice to Ahab in 1 Kgs 21:1–16. Such an association could hint in advance of Haman's downfall, though given Naboth's experience it does not yet guarantee success for Mordecai.
[26] Eccl. 10:1.
[27] Though Haman will actually be up through the night.

wisdom available to them because we live in a world that does not recognise God's authority or (frequently) even our right to claim he is at work.

This wisdom requires us to be culturally sensitive and aware of how power structures and society function, including power structures that we might regard as inimical to our faith. This is a particularly important element of cross-cultural mission where missionaries need to learn not only the local language, but also the local culture. But this is equally true within the Western world as we increasingly face the challenge of living in post-Christendom and the loss of a Christian awareness within the population at large. We do not advance the work of the kingdom by alienating people because the gospel itself must be the only stumbling block. But this does not mean that we thereby guarantee every outcome. The folly of evil will still bring challenges that we could never have perceived, just as Esther could never have guessed that the moment where it seemed she had set everything in place for the deliverance of her people would be the point where Haman would take a further step against Mordecai. This is the ambiguity of the world in which we live, one in which we know and affirm God's presence, but one where the mystery of God's presence means we do not dictate to him how and where he works. And yet, we continue to labour with all the wisdom available to us.

6:1–13
6. A funny thing happened...

The various elements that have been building within the plot come to a climax in what is the narrative centre of the book.[1] Not, of course, that all the elements of the drama have yet been resolved, but hints now emerge of how finally they will be. The threat to Mordecai's life left hanging at the end of chapter 5 is here resolved, though without any direct involvement by the Jews. That the king delights to honour Mordecai suggests he is on the rise in the Persian court. Haman however, begins to fall. How far he will fall is not yet clear, but the final words of his advisors and wife all indicate that the fall will be complete. We thus reach the point where fortunes turn, even if much needs to be resolved.

There is also a consistent hint of providence in the way the events work out. Coincidences are particularly important, though the narrative seems to hint that they are not just accidents. This does not mean that everything that happens is some massive application of divine sovereignty, since we are not robots, but it does provide a mechanism by which the book points to God's involvement. And though the book of Esther has often made use of satire, the element of humour is more pronounced here than elsewhere. Indeed, Berlin regards it as 'one of the funniest anywhere' in the Bible.[2] But the crucial point lies in the timing of events, all of which with hindsight can be seen as evidence of God's involvement, since not only do important things happen, they happen just when they are needed. Thus, on the right night to discover that Mordecai needs to be rewarded, the king cannot sleep. Similarly, Haman arrives at the court at an unconscionably early hour, but it turns out to be the

[1] See K. H. Jobes, *Esther: The NIV Application Commentary* (Grand Rapids: Zondervan, 1999), pp. 154–158, for an analysis of the literary devices creating this.
[2] A. Berlin, *Esther: The Traditional Hebrew Text with the New JPS Translation* (Philadelphia: Jewish Publication Society, 2001), p. 56.

very point at which the king needs advice about how to honour Mordecai. God's presence is unseen but no less real for that. God is present, but one can still laugh at Persian inadequacies.

1. The king's sleepless night (6:1–3)

The opening words of verse 1 (*On that night*) clearly link these events with the end of chapter 5. On the very night that Haman is busy erecting a ridiculously oversized stake on which to impale Mordecai, the king is unable to sleep. Indeed, although most translations offer something rather prosaic here such as 'the king could not sleep',[3] a more literal translation indicates that in fact 'sleep fled' from him. The cause for this nocturnal problem is not stated. A number of ancient versions corrected this perceived defect by stating explicitly that God took it from him,[4] though it would be contrary to the writer's style to state anything as directly as that. Rather, God's involvement is suggested by the timing of the king's sleeplessness, in that his sleep fled on what will turn out to be just the right night. It is the coincidence of the timing that matters, though that really is the writer's cipher for divine intervention.[5]

Of course, although the timing of the king's insomnia will turn out to be propitious, it is perfectly possible to understand why the king might not have been able to sleep. If our exegesis of 5:7–8 is correct then the king may be aware that Esther is about to (quite literally) take him up on his promise of up *to the half of [his] kingdom*. Ahasuerus might not be the brightest king that ever lived, but even for him this would be a perfectly plausible reason for sleeplessness. Nevertheless, the point highlighted is that it took place at exactly the right time. The timing is coincidental, but in that we see the work of providence. Esther's wisdom in how she came to the king will be greater than Haman's folly, but it will take something more than wisdom to deliver the Jews.

The king's response to sleeplessness was to call for the Chronicles of the kingdom to be read to him. This was the record book which had noted the time Mordecai had provided the information which prevented an assassination attempt on the king.[6] Paton objects that with so many women available this approach hardly is probable as there would certainly have been more entertaining ways

---

[3] E.g. ESV, NIV. See also Dan. 6:18.
[4] L. B. Paton provides details in *A Critical and Exegetical Commentary on the Book of Esther* (Edinburgh: T & T Clark, 1908), p. 244.
[5] D. J. A. Clines, *Ezra, Nehemiah, Esther* (Grand Rapids: Eerdmans, 1984), p. 307.
[6] 2:21–23.

to deal with the problem.[7] However, Baldwin's observation that he hoped that the droning sound of the human voice reading would put him to sleep[8] has much to commend it. Many a Christian who was perhaps a little weary at the time has found how hard it can be to stay awake during a dull sermon, and since the Chronicles of the kingdom were probably a rather boring book, rather like an extended journal of the king's daily experiences, it is easy to imagine that having it read would be somewhat soporific. So, we are probably to imagine that the king is listening to the reading of the Chronicles with the sole goal of being put to sleep. He is certainly not looking to discover anything new. Yet it is at this very point that the failure to reward Mordecai becomes apparent. As Haman is busy erecting a stake on which to have Mordecai executed, the king discovers that Mordecai has saved his life. The timing could not be better and the king is now wide awake.

We should not imagine that the passage about Mordecai was the only one read. The passive *was found* more naturally suggests that the events involving Mordecai came out simply because a passage of text, perhaps a fairly lengthy one, was read out. How long into the reading this was is not stated. It is simply said that it was found in words that virtually quote 2:21. The scandal here from Ahasuerus' point of view is that Persian kings were supposed to be particularly good at rewarding those who served them. Without saying so directly, the narrator clearly points to God's providential activity in the telling of the story. Several years have passed since Mordecai provided the information that saved the king, and yet only now, on the night Haman was preparing to have Mordecai executed, did the king discover he had not been rewarded. The king was no doubt concerned because the Chronicles should have recorded Mordecai's reward and perhaps it is the absence of any record of a reward that triggers his question to his attendants. The timing is impeccable, but only because there is more to it than meets the eye. One can almost imagine the king stuttering out the question of verse 3 in surprise since the record should not only have recorded what Mordecai has done, but also the reward and dignity bestowed upon him. The response of the servants can thus be explicit. Nothing has been done for Mordecai because nothing has been recorded. Thus, a major problem for the king has developed.

In thinking about God's providential involvement in the life of his people, it is worth noting the considerable delay between

---

[7] Paton, *A Critical and Exegetical Commentary on the Book of Esther*, p. 244.

[8] J. G. Baldwin, *Esther: An Introduction and Commentary* (Leicester: IVP, 1984), p. 89.

the time when Mordecai provided the information which saved the king's life and the time when the importance of a proper reward is noted. Esther had become queen in the seventh year of Ahasuerus' reign,[9] and it is probable that the information provided by Mordecai was close to this time, though this is not absolutely clear. Haman arranged for the order for the destruction of the Jews in Ahasuerus' twelfth year,[10] so there is presumably a gap of more than four years between when Mordecai should have been rewarded and when the issue finally came to the king's attention. It is easy to become impatient, imagining that God's providential care for his people should follow our timetable and be immediately evident. But although this chapter will show that God is active in the life of his people, it turns out that God's timetable of events is not necessarily the same as ours. Scripture provides plenty of examples of times when God's involvement is more immediate, such as the fact that it is while Ezra is still praying about the problem of mixed marriages that the people themselves begin to address the issue.[11] But there are others for whom the timing is itself part of the problem. We are told, for instance, that Hannah was provoked over many years by Peninah before God gave her the gift of a son.[12] But in both these instances the timing was right for God's purposes. Hence, one of the challenges of Christian discipleship is to live with the tension of knowing that God does act for his people, but that it may very well be at a time other than we would choose.

2. Haman traps himself (6:4–9)

While the king has been up all night, so has Haman, though their reasons have been remarkably different. Haman was up by choice, the king by a lack of sleep, but both are up as a result of providence. God's providential care is again in evidence as Haman arrived at the court at exactly the right moment to solve the king's dilemma, but in such a way as to trap himself. The scene is told with great humour as Haman gradually lowers himself into his own trap, though a trap that is full of divine coincidences. Thus, the king asks who is present to help him solve the problem just as Haman enters. That this is very early is apparent from the fact that this is the period in which the king wishes to sleep. Haman wants to ensure that he is first to see the king, as indeed he will. And both of them wish to discuss Mordecai, though for vastly different reasons.

[9] 2:16.
[10] 3:7.
[11] Ezra 10:1–5.
[12] 1 Sam. 1.

Ahasuerus has consistently needed guidance from his counsellors so, even though one might imagine he would have some idea about what to do, he responds to the news from his courtiers by asking who was in the court. Normally, the leading members of the government would be absent, with only the necessary overnight functionaries present. But in asking who is in the court Ahasuerus clearly signals that he is looking for assistance. The phrasing of verse 4 suggests that Haman was arriving even as the king posed the question of who is present. The timing is perfect. Naturally, Haman stands in the outer court, close to where Esther stood in 5:1, though the results of their visits will be very different. Haman has come to speak to the king, and in a nicely ironic touch, that also is what the king wants to do, though in the conversation that follows neither will make clear to the other the actual point of their discussion. The king never knows that Haman has come to speak to him about executing Mordecai, and of course the attendants are ignorant of this too. Hence, when confronted with a question from the king that is clearly seeking guidance the servants seize on Haman's arrival, announcing that he is standing in the outer court, waiting to see the king. From their point of view, and that of the king, nothing could be better than to have the state's leading official present at precisely the time the king needs him. Two sleepless nights are coming together, and the king accordingly summoned Haman to join him.

With the king's permission to enter, Haman duly came in. Previous encounters with the king carefully used court language,[13] and so we expect this pattern to be followed here. But the narrator has set up this expectation in order to surprise us by its absence this time as none of the normal court formalities are followed. Instead, the king immediately poses the question of what is to be done for the man he delights to honour. Haman thus will not discover about whom the king is speaking until it is too late. At this stage, the king does not distrust Haman, so the fact that Mordecai's name is not mentioned simply highlights the irony of what is taking place.[14] The king's question could, of course, be purely hypothetical, but Haman does at least recognise that a genuine reward is required. But crucially, it means Haman is thrown off his guard from the outset.

The king's question is innocent enough. It is precisely the sort of question that a trusted adviser should be able to answer. Haman presumably would know the protocols involved quite well. Nevertheless, Haman's vanity becomes his downfall. Here, the narrator breaks with the pattern of restraint that is characteristic of most of

[13] 1:16–21; 3:8–11; 5:3–4, 6–8.
[14] B. W. Anderson, 'The Book of Esther' in G. W. Buttrick (ed.), *The Interpreter's Bible* vol. 3 (Nashville: Abingdon, 1954), p. 859.

the book and shows the typical omniscience of a third person narrator, recording what Haman *said to himself*.[15] But the insight is crucial. Haman can imagine no one more worthy of reward from the king than himself. We are not told why Haman should think this, though given his position the receipt of rewards would not be unusual. But the important point is that we see how easily he is distracted from his purpose, for the whole story would have differed had he simply asked who the king had in mind. Instead, all concerns with Mordecai are put suddenly aside. Haman sees only the possibility of reward for himself, and for someone whose ego is as inflated as his there is nothing more desirable than glory and honour. The ego has landed, and the threat to Mordecai is put aside as the simple consequence of Haman not bothering to discover about whom the king is speaking.

Haman's directly reportable speech only commences in verse 7, though his opening words virtually quote the king's question back to him, as if chewing them over before speaking. A similar strategy had worked for Esther (5:7), though it may be no more than the normal court protocol. Whatever Haman's intention (and he may simply wish to savour the words), the effect is to heighten the scene's irony since the two men are thinking in completely opposite directions, stressing that this is a meeting of persons but not of minds. The answer proper therefore only begins in verse 8, though its content is somewhat surprising. Since Haman was already a man of wealth and position, typical rewards such as money, land or a title were of no interest. Instead, he describes a fantasy where he is seen as equivalent to the king, though in reality the nature of the reward would be known only to the king and his immediate circle.[16] This is particularly apparent in Haman's desire for clothing worn by the king and a chance to ride one of the king's own horses. Although they would evidently be status goods, the general public could hardly know who owned them. Hence, the show is more for Haman's own personal enjoyment than anything else, a chance to be dressed up as if he is the king and nothing more, but with the added twist that the other nobles of the Empire should be brought in to play the game too by proclaiming that this was the king's way of honouring someone. For the nobles it would be clear that Haman was the most important person in the kingdom, though for anyone else the meaning of such a reward would be rather hard to discern. Some commentators believe that Haman is virtually claiming the

[15] Literally, 'said in his heart'.
[16] There are obvious similarities to Joseph's reward from Pharaoh (Gen. 41:42–43), except there it is clear that Joseph remains entirely subservient to Pharaoh, and of course Joseph's honour is appropriate.

kingdom here,[17] but since the honour still requires public affirmation of the king's own authority this probably reads in slightly more than is intended.

There is a small syntactic problem in verse 8 about where the crown is to be placed, but the best option is probably that the royal crown is on the head of the horse.[18] If so, the horse's headdress may be a means of indicating that this is a royal horse, somewhat akin to the flags placed on the cars of heads of state in motorcades. Although this may seem odd, there is inscriptional material from Assyria showing some form of headdress on horses that supports such a reading, and this practice could have continued in Persia.[19] Yet, unconsciously, Haman sets himself up for his fall, and will be trapped by his own words,[20] particularly his insistence that the clothes should be given to one of the king's most senior officials.[21] Haman clearly means any other senior official but himself, but his own foolish speech will trap him in ways he cannot have considered. But from the narrator's point of view Haman's speech is precisely how he traps himself. God's timing has created the opportunity for Haman's demise, and precisely at the point where Haman imagines himself at the highest point he has in reality begun to fall.

3. Mordecai honoured, Haman falling (6:10–13)

The king's response to Haman is delicious in its irony. Haman is immediately instructed to carry out his suggestion, with the careful reminder that he is to do everything he has said without fail. The garment, the horse and all that is required must not only be provided, but all must be done quickly, perhaps because of the previous delay in honouring Mordecai. The king's commands are issued directly to Haman so he must personally ensure all is done without fail. The idiom employed by the king here (literally letting 'nothing fall'[22]) echoes Joshua 21:45; 23:14 and 1 Samuel 3:19. There it refers to the certainty of God's word fulfilling its purpose, and

---

[17] E.g. Berlin, *Esther: The Traditional Hebrew Text with the New JPS Translation*, pp. 60–61.

[18] So ESV.

[19] M. V. Fox, *Character and Ideology in the Book of Esther* (2nd ed., Grand Rapids: Eerdmans, 2001), p. 77. C. A. Moore, in *Esther* (Garden City: Doubleday, 1971), Plate 2, shows Persian reliefs to demonstrate this, but they do not clearly show a crown.

[20] Prov. 18:7. Similarly, T. S. Laniak, 'Esther', in L. C. Allen and T. S. Laniak, *Ezra, Nehemiah, Esther* (Peabody: Hendrickson, 2003), p. 239.

[21] Cf. Prov. 10:14; 14:3; 18:7.

[22] ESV 'Leave out nothing'. The verb 'to fall' (*nāpal*) is also a theme word through the chapter, and here contrasts with the certainty of Haman's own fall in 6:13.

just as God's word does not fail,[23] so Haman must ensure that he carries out all he has said. But it is the sentence's structure that builds the irony. Haman is told to do all that he has said, even to the extent of having his suggestions quoted back at him, for Mordecai. Mordecai's name is introduced at the last moment possible, so that Haman's shock at not being the one honoured is revealed as late as possible. The effect is made all the more dramatic when the king specifically refers to Mordecai as *the Jew who sits at the king's gate*. Huey finds it odd that the king should wish to honour a Jew so soon after issuing a decree for their destruction,[24] but this is a king who is particularly good at not knowing things, so he does not see the contradiction in his actions. For Haman, however, this would be remarkably clear. The irony is thus entirely for the reader to enjoy, but not for Haman who has no choice but to obey.

The narrative then records Haman's obedience in this in verse 11, though it refrains from psychologising the experience for either Haman or Mordecai.[25] Haman must take the garment and horse and follow through on the king's command, though with one minor alteration. Where Haman had imagined a group of nobles placing the honouree on the horse, it is only Haman who places Mordecai there. There are clearly limits to the indignity he is able to face even if he still had to walk through the square personally announcing that this was what was done for *the man whom the king delights to honour*. In doing this, it is Haman who changes Mordecai's garments from sackcloth, something Mordecai had earlier refused to do for Esther.[26] Now, just as Esther has put on royalty,[27] so also Mordecai is dressed royally. The irony is far more important than the psychology of Haman and Mordecai through these events, though it must have galled Haman to grant Mordecai the honour he craved. Indeed, Mordecai is entirely passive throughout, and simply returns to his habitual abode of the palace gate. By contrast, Haman hurried home mourning (the same word in 4:1, 3 describes the Jews), and with his head covered as a sign of this.[28] The extent of his mourning is not developed further because readers can already see the beginning of the reversal of fortunes between Haman and Mordecai in a neatly ironic way.

---

[23] Isa. 55:11.

[24] F. B. Huey, 'Esther', in F. E. Gaebelein (ed.), *The Expositor's Bible Commentary*, vol. 4 (Grand Rapids: Zondervan, 1988), p. 823.

[25] Though it has not stopped generations of interpreters from the Talmud and on from doing so – see J. Carruthers, *Esther through the Ages* (Oxford: Blackwell, 2008), pp. 227–232.

[26] L. M. Day, *Esther* (Nashville: Abingdon, 2005), p. 111.

[27] 5:1.

[28] 2 Sam. 15:30.

Far more important to the narrator is that Haman again gathered his friends (here teasingly called his *wise men*) and wife to recount his experiences. This time there is no boasting. Instead, he can describe only the humiliation that has befallen him. The answer they give offers no comfort. This time, though, it is his friends who take the lead whereas last time it was Zeresh. Nevertheless, they are agreed that if Mordecai is Jewish, then there is no hope for Haman. He must fall. No reason is directly given for this, but it indicates that even the oppressors recognise the providence the chapter as a whole portrays. Perhaps there is an allusion here to the promise of Israel destroying Amalek (Exod. 17:16), though the fact that Mordecai is literally said to be of the 'seed of the Jews'[29] might also be suggestive. The word 'seed' is particularly important in the promise to Abraham[30] and David,[31] and both these texts emphasise God's commitment to his people. In addition, the narrative so far has reminded us of the ancient conflict between Israel and Amalek, a conflict which is ultimately to be won by Israel.[32] The Persians might not know the passages well enough to quote them, but the narrator gives a nod towards them in quoting the Persians. What Persians might see as only an unexplainable element about Jewish survival is in reality a truth that is grounded in Scripture, and beyond that in the faithfulness of God. Something inscrutable to those who do not know God becomes explicable for those who know him through his Word. A further irony is also implicit, since Haman's friends and wife effectively deny knowledge of Mordecai's descent, even though Haman made it clear in 5:14. Here though, the fear that perhaps lurks behind anti-Semitism is given a clear voice.

Throughout the chapter, the author has thus hinted at God's presence. In and of themselves coincidences are unremarkable. But it is the form the coincidences take that suggests something more is happening here than might otherwise meet the eye. The king cannot sleep on the right night, and on that night he discovers a four-year-old error. When he needs advice (and this is a king who never acts without advice, even as he accepts all the advice he is given) who should be present but Haman? Haman has come at exactly the right moment to arrange Mordecai's execution, but at the crucial point is distracted from his quest by his own pride. Although the ensuing conversation has elements that might seem more at home in a slapstick comedy, it all points to a greater hand that is involved, and that is the hand of God that works in the unseen and often quite

[29] ESV 'of the Jewish people'.
[30] Gen. 15:3, 5, 13, 18; 17:7–10, 12, 19.
[31] 2 Sam. 7:12; 22:51.
[32] Exod. 17:16; Num. 24:20; Deut. 25:17–19; 1 Sam. 15:2–8.

unspectacular ways of daily life. Further, these coincidences are not empty events in and of themselves. Rather, they point to the process which has now begun whereby the Jews' fortunes are being reversed. The reality of this reversal is something that even Haman's confidants are able to recognise, for they see in Mordecai's Jewish background the reason for the events that have been taking place. God is thus active even where initially he cannot be seen – active in what appears to be nothing more than the mundane processes of normal life. In our own time, with our modern emphasis upon the spectacular, that is a point that is well worth pondering. God can work through the miraculous, but more often it is through something far simpler. We need, perhaps, to develop the skill of reflecting more on the seemingly ordinary events of life to appreciate how God has been at work in our daily experience. This is often in ways that we only notice at a later point when we recognise how a series of apparently unconnected events actually come together to serve the purposes of God. What is crucial here is that the coincidences happen when Mordecai and Esther have committed themselves to God and his people. But there is certainly a sense here that when God's people commit themselves to his purposes, as Esther and Mordecai have, then such coincidences are that much more frequent. At the same time, this is an important reminder that, although we are called to be wise in all our dealings with the world, wisdom alone is not enough. We always need the extra that God brings, but we need to be open to the fact that this extra may have come through a chain of seemingly minor events whose significance is only seen when we look back on them.

6:14 – 7:10
7. An awkward dinner

The events of 6:1–13 have all happened without any direct input from Esther, yet they fundamentally prepare for how everything begins to come together in this chapter. Esther finally reveals the purpose behind her banquets and Haman finally falls, fulfilling what was said by his advisers and wife at 6:13. There is, of course, a profound irony in that he is impaled upon the stake he had erected for Mordecai. Perhaps even more ironic is that although he is clearly guilty of planning genocide he is actually executed for the crime of rape even though he has not committed it – unless coming too close to the queen is deemed equivalent to this. But this irony has other levels operative because in his proposal for rewarding himself he had played out the fantasy of being virtually equivalent to the king, which presumably could also have meant close contact with the queen. There are accordingly multiple levels of irony in the text. Yet even with these levels of irony, the narrative is aware of texts like Proverbs 26:27 which assert that our actions have unseen consequences which come back on us.[1] As Paul puts it, what we sow from our sinful nature will 'reap corruption'[2] and Haman here reaps what he sows in terms of the final outcome. However, the chapter also demonstrates that achieving a personal goal is not enough – Esther needs to go beyond Haman's unmasking because there is a greater matter involved than simply ensuring the downfall of an adversary to God's people.

Once again, the narrator is not particularly interested in details of characterisation. These elements are left to the reader to imply and we return to the technique, which dominates the book, of not knowing much more than the characters. The insight of what

[1] This can also be the basis for prayer, as in Pss. 7:16–17; 17:13; 109:6–19.
[2] Gal. 6:8.

Haman thought in 6:6 remains the notable exception. We do not know, for example, why Esther does not intervene on Haman's behalf concerning the crime with which he is charged, nor do we know what motivates the eunuch Harbona to point out the presence of the stake Haman had erected, though his additional note indicating that it was built for Mordecai may suggest he represents a group in the palace opposed to Haman. Such elements are left to one side. We know only the process that leads to Haman's death and that it finally subdues the king's anger. Even so, we do not know precisely *why* the king was angry at Esther's revelation. A number of factors come into play, but it is not the narrative's intention to answer these questions, and so our focus must be on those matters the text does want us to address.

1. Unmasking Haman (6:14 – 7:6)

The narrative provides no gap between the final words of Haman's friends and the arrival of the king's eunuchs. Indeed, it was while Haman was still speaking with his friends that the eunuchs arrived to hurry him to the dinner, meaning that even if his friends or Zeresh had any positive advice there is no opportunity for it to be given. Since the second banquet takes place on the same day as the events that befell Haman the fact of the timing is not particularly surprising, but that he was not yet ready for the eunuchs may suggest he is losing control of the flow of events. The advice for the erection of the stake for Mordecai's execution and visit to the king all indicated that he believed he controlled his own destiny, though the events of the previous chapter have totally undermined that confidence. Something more than human intervention was required to enable the coincidences that led to him being the one to honour Mordecai rather than executing him. The element of a lack of control may also be suggested by the fact that eunuchs hurried him to the banquet. Since Esther has already prepared the banquet it could be that they hurry him because he is an important guest and it cannot begin without him,[3] but even so he no longer controls events as before. Indeed, being hurried like this looks more like how someone is arrested than brought to a banquet. Whether the implication is that in conversation Haman had forgotten to prepare himself[4] or that it is simply a convention of the court that the king is not to be kept waiting and haste is therefore important,[5] it is

[3] So C. A. Moore, *Esther* (Garden City: Doubleday, 1971), p. 69.
[4] J. G. Baldwin, *Esther: An Introduction and Commentary* (Leicester: IVP, 1984), p. 91.
[5] D. J. A. Clines, *Ezra, Nehemiah, Esther* (Grand Rapids: Eerdmans, 1984), p. 310.

apparent that Haman's control is slipping. He is accordingly brought to the banquet rather than one who simply comes. Although we are told that both the king and Haman came to the banquet Esther had prepared, it is clear that they have come in very different ways.

Verse 2 provides the king with the opportunity to again ask the question of Esther he had posed in 5:6. As with the second offer on the previous day, it was *as they were drinking wine after the feast*[6] that Ahasuerus tried to discover what Esther sought. This is particularly important for him since in terms of Esther's response in 5:8 he now stands the very real risk of being forced to give up half his kingdom. But it also shows Esther's patience, as even with the virtual guarantee on the previous day she still had to wait for the king to initiate the offer. That the offer of *even to the half of my kingdom* is an important element for Ahasuerus may be hinted at in his use of the formal title 'Queen Esther', something omitted at the previous dinner. In spite of this, he continues to express himself as before, offering Esther up to half the kingdom, though with the obvious wish that she will not take him seriously.

The narrator also emphasises Esther's status at the meal, calling her 'Queen Esther' as if to echo the honour offered to her by the king. As before, Esther's answer is carefully structured, only raising issues obliquely.[7] The king expressed his request in two parts, so Esther indicates two matters that she seeks from him, though the two are intimately related to one another. But she is first careful to express herself in appropriate court language, again using two *if* clauses, whilst addressing the king in the appropriately formal and indirect manner. Initially she uses a more direct address (*your sight*) before moving to the more traditional third person style. The two conditions are essentially formal though, for we know that Esther has already found favour (*ḥēn*) with the king, and to date no suggestion has been made that has failed to please the king. Nevertheless, it is still appropriate to answer in a manner that displays the appropriate attitude to the monarch, especially one as volatile as Ahasuerus when he has had a bit to drink. But the measured language with which Esther begins is rapidly replaced in the second half of verse 3 with much more passionate terms. It is almost as if the effort of keeping her emotions in check has proved to be too much. Hence, although she still echoes the terms of the king's offer by speaking of her *wish* and her *request* her speech becomes much terser as she asks for her life as her request and that of her people as

---

[6] Lit. 'during the banquet of wine'.
[7] As does Nathan, 2 Sam. 12:1–6.

her petition. Coming out as suddenly as it does, it left the king without much detail as to why she makes the request she does. There is no particular reason to believe at this stage that the king would associate Esther's request with Haman's earlier actions. Nevertheless, Haman would know. In this is the paradox of Esther's situation. In seeking for her life she must reveal her ethnicity for the first time, and thus place her life at risk.[8]

The opening *for* of verse 4 then provides the reason for Esther's otherwise somewhat unusual request. Her people have been *sold* to destruction and it is this fact that generates her request. By wisely using the passive *sold* (*mkr*) Esther delicately sidesteps any direct mention of the king's role in enabling the decree against her people. After all, it is seldom wise to challenge an autocrat though, perhaps more importantly, Haman had played on the king's ignorance and the ease with which he could be led. A direct accusation against the king would thus distract everyone from the central issue, so again we see Esther's wisdom in choosing her words. Even in distress, though, Esther's reference to her people being *sold* hints at the bribe Haman had offered the king for their destruction, though it is sometimes used to refer to certain destruction without any financial element.[9] Indeed, Esther goes on to quote directly from Haman's decree, noting that her people were to be *destroyed ... killed and ... annihilated.* The king may not, at this stage, recognise exactly what is going on apart from the fact that there is an attempt on the queen's life. But by quoting the decree and by using such a loaded word as *sold* Esther was raising the stakes by revealing to Haman how much she knew of his plot. Esther thus neatly illustrates the important point that the one set of words can have two very different meanings for those who hear them. The king has been told that a decree has been issued against her people, though they are still unnamed, but, even though he has never been addressed, Esther has also told Haman that she knows he is the one behind it all. Those who are called upon to pray in public are usually aware that their words are heard differently in that, although they are directed to God, they can also act to inform or challenge the congregation. The reality is that words carefully chosen for one hearer will be heard differently by others, which is perhaps why the book of Proverbs so often encourages wise speech so that righteous words can be a 'fountain of life'[10] in a variety of settings.

The last part of verse 4 is unfortunately very difficult, and can be interpreted in a number of ways. Esther clearly asserts that had her

[8] Clines, *Ezra, Nehemiah, Esther*, p. 311.
[9] Judg. 2:14.
[10] Prov. 10:11.

people only been sold into slavery she would have remained silent; the difficulty is in determining her reason for acting in this way. Slavery, she asserts, would not have justified bothering the king. The difficulty lies in determining the particular nuance to be assigned to the words *ṣār* and *šōweh*. Both pose problems for interpreters since *ṣār* could mean either 'adversary' or 'distress', while the participle *šōweh* most commonly has the meaning of 'being even', though such a meaning is hardly appropriate here, and it is more likely that Esther is speaking of an equivalence of some sort.[11] But what is that equivalence? If we take *ṣār* to mean 'enemy', then the sense of the phrase would appear to be that Haman could not offset the damage caused to the king, perhaps because of the loss in taxation. Effectively, Esther would be claiming that the bribe could not cover the longer term loss. But if Esther means 'distress' then she is saying that the affliction caused to her people would not be sufficient to trouble to king if they were sold into slavery. Since she is particularly concerned with the needs of her people this is perhaps more probable, and certainly provides a more cogent argument for silence, though it is probably an ironic understatement on her part intended simply to affirm the Jews' loyalty to the state.[12] The fact that she is speaking therefore suggests a situation far more dire than that of slavery. By leaving her statement at that point Esther virtually forces the king to discover the reason for such words. It is doubtful that he remembers the earlier decree, and his question of verse 5 certainly suggests that he was still ignorant of what was really happening. Wisdom here involves knowing when to pause so that, rather than simply telling the king everything, he is drawn in to find out what Esther means.

The king's answer in verse 5 is notable for its double use of 'he said', only the second of which actually introduces direct speech, which is perhaps why it is omitted in most English versions.[13] Whilst a doubling of verbs associated with speech is common enough, repeating same verb is unusual though not without parallel, and suggests the king's stuttering surprise.[14] This effect is retained by the phrasing of his questions. Once again there are two of them since the king does not seem capable of asking anything only once. The questions themselves are simple and direct, and sound rather

[11] D. Reid suggests possible deliberate ambiguity, in *Esther: An Introduction and Commentary* (Nottingham: IVP, 2008), pp. 125–126.

[12] See A. Berlin, *Esther: The Traditional Hebrew Text with the New JPS Translation* (Philadelphia: Jewish Publication Society, 2001), pp. 66–67, though she prefers to see this is an accusation of treason by Haman.

[13] This translation tradition reaches back to LXX.

[14] Cf. Gen. 22:7.

like the comments of someone struggling to control their surprise. His comment is thus that of someone who does not know what is happening. What is clear is that Ahasuerus knows that someone has dared to do this,[15] and so what he wants to know who and where this person is. The irony of the king's ignorance to this point is thus beautifully played out. Haman, of course, knows he is the one being discussed, but he is a bystander in a conversation over which he has no control. Indeed, the narrator never mentions anything said by Haman throughout this meal, a marked contrast to earlier passages where he is invariably loquacious. His loss of power is thus demonstrated within the narrative. He is now an object of the conversation of others, but no longer one who initiates and controls events. His fall is not yet complete, but the comment by his friends[16] on the certainty of his fall before Mordecai is already demonstrated by this.

By drawing the king to find out what was happening Esther can finally accuse Haman directly in verse 6. Once again she stalls slightly in making her request, first making clear the evil nature of the adversary before she names him as Haman. The piling up of negative terms, describing Haman as a *foe*[17] *and enemy* before naming him as *This wicked Haman* heightens the presentation of his crime. Up to this point, Haman has been a bystander to the proceedings. He could no doubt see how events were drawing round him, but with the full revelation of his position he now comes back into the centre of the narrative, but only at a point where he can do nothing to affect his circumstances. He can only be terrified as he sits in the presence of the king and queen, knowing that it is his plan, and accordingly his fate, that is being discussed. But his terror is thoroughly understandable given the impetuous ways Ahasuerus could act.

2. Dealing with the king's anger (7:7–10)

Haman may be terrified, but as soon as he is named we see the king's anger. The king's anger has been mentioned twice before, in 1:12 when he initiated the process to remove Vashti and again in 2:1 when he remembered what he had done to her as his anger abated. Since then we have also had two mentions of Haman's anger, in 3:5 where he is initially angered by Mordecai and then again in 5:9

[15] Literally, 'filled his heart', but the heart is often an organ of volition in the Old Testament.
[16] 6:13.
[17] Esther plays on the sense of ṣār, focusing on Haman as the enemy rather than on the sense of 'distress' used earlier.

before agreeing to arrange for Mordecai's execution. The previous references have all shown the danger that self-centred anger generates attacking others without considering other factors. This passage also has two references to anger, as it is triggered by Esther's naming of Haman and as it abates once the problem of Haman is resolved.[18] The king is as impetuous as ever, but this time his anger is related to a genuine abuse, though it would over-simplify matters to regard this as righteous anger since Ahasuerus has clearly been taken for a fool by Haman. Esther however has at least enabled anger which can bring about change. The Bible recognises the danger brought by anger and generally warns against it,[19] but acknowledges that there were times when even Jesus was angry[20] and that sometimes controlled anger will be needed for a short time in dealing with sin.[21] We do not know the cause of the king's anger – he could have been angry that there was a plan against the life of the queen, or that Haman was involved or perhaps that he now realised he had unwittingly been a part of the whole event. The source of Ahasuerus' anger is not stated, and though it is not controlled, it is at least partially directed against sin.

Ahasuerus' anger also serves an important narrative purpose as he then withdrew from the main room for a period. The king's retreat to the garden provides Haman with the opportunity to plead *for his life from Queen Esther*. Earlier, the root *bqš* had been used to describe Esther's *request* before the king. The verbal form of this root is now employed as Haman seeks mercy from Esther. The irony of the situation, asking for mercy from his intended victim, was probably lost on Haman. He could see how dangerous his situation was since the king plainly intended to do something about him, though exactly what is unclear. Presumably, it is also unclear to the king at this time, since he has no one to advise him how he should act against his chief adviser. However, Haman apparently perceives that the *harm* the king intends to do him could be fatal since the verb *kālâ* frequently has the sense of taking of someone's life. Hence, Haman pleads for his life. In spite of all these indications, it is also apparent that the king has not resolved his anger, and determining the form the resolution will take is apparently what he is doing in the garden.

As with the events of chapter 6, the resolution of Ahasuerus' anger occurs through a coincidence of timing. We are not told if he had decided what to do, but he returns to the room at precisely the

---

[18] 7:7, 10.
[19] Prov. 15:1, 18; 20:2; 27:4; 30:33; Gal. 5:20; Eph. 6:4; Col. 3:8; Jas 1:19–20.
[20] Mark 3:5.
[21] Eph. 4:26.

point when Haman falls before Esther to beg for his life. The irony is that it is pleading for his life that costs Haman his life. More particularly, Haman is falling on the couch where Esther is reclining as the king enters. The action normally involved falling at the feet of the person to whom the request is made – and since a standard idiom is used Haman is clearly not attempting to rape Esther. The king's response is excessive, though it may be another example of the king being unknowing. However we construe his response there can be no doubt that accusing Haman of rape would neatly solve his problem since he can hardly charge him of his actual crime without bringing himself into disrepute. Although the verb *kābaš* does not necessarily mean 'rape' – more commonly meaning 'subdue' – it is clear that this is the accusation made against Haman. As a charge it is absurd – not only because Haman is following a standard custom, but also because of the improbability that Haman would try to rape the queen when he is already in deep trouble with the king. Haman's timing is impeccably bad, though the Targum emphasises the element of God's providence by having an angel push Haman at that time. Many commentators accuse Esther of being hard-hearted here, since she knows that the charge against Haman is false.[22] However, the nature of Persian law makes it impossible for Esther to act otherwise since the king's words are virtually a decree against Haman.[23] In any case, by approaching Esther like this Haman has violated harem etiquette, so there is little that can be done for him.[24] Esther's silence may not be a model of piety, but it is at least understandable in the circumstances!

As a result of the king's declaration, Haman's face is covered. No reason is given for this, and parallels that have been cited are on the whole less than clear and helpful, but the decisive change is that in 6:12 he had covered it to show his own mourning. Now, he is entirely at the king's disposal, though the servants there apparently needed no direct order to cover Haman's head, acting directly on the king's accusation. No decision has yet been made about his future, but it seems he is already being treated as a condemned man. In any case, it is notable that the king only acts once he perceives a threat to himself. Such kings are always dangerous! The king does not, however, seem to have any plan that will enable him to deal with Haman, and it is only when Harbona, one of the king's

---

[22] E.g., B. W. Anderson, 'The Book of Esther' in G. W. Buttrick (ed.), *The Interpreter's Bible* vol. 3 (Nashville: Abingdon, 1954), p. 862.

[23] , J. G. Baldwin, *Esther*, p. 93.

[24] Note that in 2 Sam. 3:7–11; 16:20–22 and 1 Kgs 2:13–25 even the possibility of a sexual relationship with a royal concubine was regarded as a claim on the throne.

personal eunuchs,[25] points out the presence of the stake, presumably visible from the palace, that Haman had erected for Mordecai that anything can happen. Harbona puts one further nail in Haman's coffin when he points out that Haman erected the stake for Mordecai *whose word saved the king*. Any hope of a reasonable defence for Haman fades at this point. When the king then orders that Haman be impaled on it he utters the final irony because those are the words Haman hoped to hear about Mordecai. Haman is hoist by his own petard as he is impaled upon his own stake, and thus is the king's anger able to abate.

As with chapter 5, there is a strong contrast here between Esther and Haman especially through the contrast of wise woman and fool which continues as before. But this contrast is also linked to more hints that God is at work behind the scenes in all that is happening. Esther's wisdom has been carefully applied, but even with Haman's folly it could not have resolved itself with so impetuous a king without something more going on. But Haman's sins do find him out as he ends up impaled on the stake he had erected for Mordecai. None of this could have happened quite as it did without the coincidences of the previous chapter, so that even as the story continues to deconstruct all human pretence at power (the king after all condemns Haman for a crime he did not commit) it continues to hint at a better option, though without ever going beyond what the characters within this story can actually see. This theological restraint is important because, by holding back, we as readers are called to ponder these events more carefully, even as Esther's own restraint in the process of identifying Haman to Ahasuerus also called him to further reflection. And as we reflect further, we appreciate that, although wickedness can seem to be about to prevail, stories such as this also give us hints of the change that God will one day bring, a change which is already revealed in the gospel. Moreover, just as the removal of Haman does not remove the evil he has initiated, but requires further action, so the gospel is an assertion of what God has done, and a promise of what he will do, which also calls us to action because of it.

The challenge for many today is to hold the balance that this passage lays before us between divine sovereignty and human responsibility. I once saw a sign in a church that asserted that 'God has no hands except ours'. The intent was clearly to encourage believers to action, to live out the demands of our faith in terms of social justice – a matter of great interest here. But the problem with such a view is that it has too small a view of God, and surely many

[25] 1:10.

of us have discovered that God has been present at points and in ways we could not have predicted. The opposite extreme was reputedly expressed by J. R. Ryland when William Carey had expressed his case for the importance of global mission at a minister's meeting in 1786: 'Young man, sit down; when God pleases to convert the heathen, he will do it without your aid and mine.' Whether or not Ryland actually said this, it is a view which reflects the opinions of some who so stress God's sovereignty that no human involvement is required. This passage shows instead that human responsibility and divine sovereignty go together.[26] In terms that Carey understood well, it is as we attempt great things for God that we can expect great things from God.[27]

---

[26] Readers interested in exploring this issue further would do well to begin with D. A. Carson, *Divine Sovereignty and Human Responsibility: Biblical Perspectives in Tension* (London: Marshall, Morgan & Scott, 1981).

[27] Carey's famous sermon may have put this differently since he may have said, 'Accept great things from God; attempt great things for God' (the quote has come down in variant forms), but this is simply to approach this balance from a slightly different angle.

8:1–17
8. Revoking the irrevocable

Haman's downfall in chapter 7 did not resolve the problem the Jews as a people faced. His downfall is a hint that the greater problem can be resolved, but the resolution so far is only in terms of the conflict between Haman and Mordecai, though Haman's death is perhaps also symbolic of God's promise to overcome Amalek.[1] The problem of the decree against the Jews still stands. Haman's downfall does not change this essential factor. Complicating matters is the fact that Persian law is not to be revoked, quite apart from the problem of a king who is not especially trustworthy. The preliminary problem of Haman has been solved, but the major crisis remains unsolved. Thus, this part of the story points to the need to move beyond personal agendas to address major systemic problems. It was never enough for Esther to remove Haman. The commitment Esther embodied in 4:15–16 was to her people and their need, not simply to guarantee her own survival. Hence, the question is raised of how the systemic evil unleashed by Haman's decree could be addressed.

The means of that resolution are set before us in this chapter, though the events that mark that resolution are only recorded in 9:1–19. However, those events need the prior intervention of Mordecai and Esther. It is notable here that Mordecai again comes to the fore. Esther established the means by which he may approach the king and deal with the issue, but once that is achieved it is Mordecai who is the dominant figure. With Mordecai's rise in status we should note that the motif of the reversal of fortunes between Mordecai and Haman reaches its logical conclusion, as Mordecai not only takes over Haman's position, but acts in the same manner

[1] Exod. 17:14.

to reverse the decree Haman had issued.[2] Here again is a hint of the hope for the Jews that will be manifest in the following chapter.

1. The elevation of Mordecai (8:1–2)

The timing of Mordecai's elevation coincides with Haman's fall. The chronological note in verse 1 (*On that day*) clearly links the two events so that Haman's execution provided Esther with the opportunity to introduce Mordecai as her relative. But along with this, we note that Haman's estate is passed on to Esther. That Haman is the villain of the piece is again highlighted by describing him as *the enemy of the Jews*. Although this fits the dominant pattern of his characterisation, in executing him Ahasuerus had also effectively declared him to be his personal enemy and thus an enemy of the Empire. Calling him the *enemy of the Jews* provides a means to re-orient the narrative away from Ahasuerus' concerns and back to the pressing issue of Haman's decree against the Jews. Herodotus notes that the property of a traitor was confiscated by the state in Persia,[3] so it is clear that the king's treatment of Haman is focused on his perceived assault on Esther. Esther's task is thus to find a means by which to re-orient the king in the same way, because from Ahasuerus' perspective the issue of Haman is resolved by the confiscation of his estate. Esther thus has a delicate issue to work through because she still cannot implicate the king directly in the planned pogrom, but her commitment to her people requires that she address the issue. However, Haman's removal provides the opportunity to introduce Mordecai to the king, which was a wise move in that the king no longer had a prime minister to advise him, and Mordecai's value to him has already been established. Hence, before we are told what Esther did with the property, we again need to be introduced to Mordecai. More importantly, he needs to be presented to the king, which is what Esther does. In doing so, she reveals *what he was to her*. This is presumably more than just introducing him as her guardian. Rather, it would suggest something of the whole nature of their relationship, perhaps even indicating something of Mordecai's part in exposing Haman.

Mordecai's presentation to the king prepares for verse 2, where both the king and Esther honour him. First, the king hands over the signet ring he has apparently removed from Haman. Giving Mordecai the ring elevates him to Haman's position, whilst also

---

[2] On the importance of this motif for the book as a whole, see S. B. Berg, *The Book of Esther: Motifs, Themes and Structure* (Missoula: Scholar's Press, 1979), pp. 106–113.

[3] 3:128–129.

granting him an honour appropriate to his previous service of the king. Esther's act of honour is a neat parallel in that she sets him over Haman's estate. Mordecai accordingly now controls all that was Haman's, illustrating the principle enunciated by Hannah[4] that God raises the poor from the ash heap and seats them with princes. Indeed, Hannah's Song[5] celebrates the ways in which God brings about a reversal of fortunes for the weak. Its particularly close parallel with Mordecai's experience suggests reference to it may be one of the ways the narrator highlights the key theological themes of this story, though here that reversal of fortunes still required the absolute commitment of God's people. Moreover, Mordecai's elevation therefore points to the possibility of a resolution for all the Jews, though this would still require considerable effort. Interestingly enough, although it is the king who formally advances Mordecai, in reality it is still Esther who causes it to happen.[6] There is therefore a further area of balance attained for the rest of the chapter – Mordecai can now initiate the process of deliverance for his people, but only because Esther is the power behind the throne, though all of this is equally dependent on God's otherwise unseen involvement.

2. Esther's intercession (8:3–8)

Verse 3 clearly begins a new scene, though one that closely parallels Esther's previous audience with the king in 5:1–4. That Esther spoke to the king once again does not necessarily mean that she has placed her life at risk[7] as she did there since she is already in the king's presence. Rather, *again* is an idiom that indicates a new phase of direct speech, adding to what has gone before.[8] That this takes place at the same time as her second feast shows Esther's solidarity with her people. Haman's downfall was only the beginning, and the full purpose of Esther's feasts can now be realised.[9] In falling at the king's feet Esther expresses her emotional involvement with her people: she is not simply acting in the appropriate court manner. This is apparent from the fact that the verb used is not employed

[4] 1 Sam. 2:8.

[5] 1 Sam. 2:1–10.

[6] J. G. McConville, *Ezra, Nehemiah, Esther* (Edinburgh: St Andrew's Press, 1985), p. 187.

[7] Contra L. B. Paton, *A Critical and Exegetical Commentary on the Book of Esther* (Edinburgh: T & T Clark, 1908), p. 269.

[8] C. A. Moore, *Esther* (Garden City: Doubleday, 1971), p. 77; D. J. A. Clines, *Ezra, Nehemiah, Esther* (Grand Rapids: Eerdmans, 1984), p. 314.

[9] J. G. Baldwin, *Esther: An Introduction and Commentary* (Leicester: IVP, 1984), p. 95.

elsewhere for doing obeisance. In addition, that Esther is crying suggests we are no longer in a formal court setting, though the fact that she pleaded with the king to avert Haman's *evil plan*[10] means she knows that it is still the king who must make the decision to act for the Jews. Characterising Haman as *the Agagite* returns to his introduction,[11] highlighting once again that he belongs to a people in perennial conflict with Israel, a conflict that needs to be overcome. That this is not simply a personal conflict is emphasised by the reference to his plot against the Jews. The issue is thus one affecting an entire people, and the king as the defender of all his peoples needs to acknowledge this. The king's decision to extend the sceptre must accordingly be interpreted as an act of encouragement to her. It thus provides the opportunity to begin to move towards countermanding Haman's decree, for although Mordecai now has the king's ring he needs the king's permission to use it.

Extending the sceptre allows Esther the opportunity to speak, but it is still something that needs to be done with care. Hence, Esther reverts to the more formal speech of the court, structuring her statement around a pair of 'if' clauses that allow the king the opportunity to conclude that the decision is still his. But following court style is not enough, because Esther has the delicate task of leading the king to see the appropriateness of her request. Thus, her first 'if' has only one condition – that what follows might *please the king*. This is open ended and could lead to rejection (though it is the same way she has initiated requests previously),[12] which is why her second 'if' has three conditions – that Esther has found favour with the king, that the matter is deemed appropriate by him and that Esther herself is pleasing to him. The middle condition here mirrors the initial point of the first clause, but sets it in the context of the king's own relationship to Esther. We know that Esther has previously found favour with the king[13] but it is important this time that the king's relationship to Esther be emphasised, because the reason Esther gives for the king's action is dependent upon her relationship to her people. She cannot bear their calamity, their coming destruction, though by phrasing these points as questions she again invites the king to reflect on the decree's impact on her. She is obviously aware that an argument based on the moral wrong of Haman's decree is unlikely to succeed.[14] But by linking the king to herself in this way she also highlights the king's relationship to

[10] Cf. 4:8.
[11] 3:1.
[12] 5:4, 8; 7:3.
[13] 2:17; 5:2.
[14] L. M. Day, *Esther* (Nashville: Abingdon, 2005), p. 133.

her people. Esther thus presents herself as the bridge joining the king and the Jews as one of his people precisely because they are Esther's people. But since one never suggests to the king exactly what he should do, Esther uses the passive *an order be written* to retain the impersonal feel. Nevertheless, it indicates clearly what the king should do. It is notable, though, that Esther goes further here than in verse 3. There she had asked the king to avert Haman's evil, but now she formally asks him to revoke his plan. Asking the king to avert Haman's decree is technically something that cannot be done since Persian law cannot be revoked.[15] Esther may, however, suggest that Haman's decree does not have this force since she refers instead to *letters* he devised for the destruction of the Jews. That the king has a personal responsibility for them is then emphasised by noting that they are in all the king's provinces. It is clear that Esther's concern is now with her people, the need that she first took up at 7:4. Her own safety, and that of Mordecai, is not enough.

The king's answer to Esther and Mordecai[16] (who has otherwise been outside the action so far) basically denies responsibility though it does permit Esther and Mordecai to act if they can. He indicates that he has handed over Haman's estate to Esther and had Haman impaled, implying this is all he can do.[17] Of course, he is not exactly truthful in claiming Haman was executed for attempting to kill the Jews since the actual accusation was raping Esther,[18] but phrasing it like this enables him to claim he has acted. This is also the first time the king shows an explicit awareness of the situation of the Jews, meaning he finally knows the people who were to be destroyed. The king can thus see nothing else he can do, but he does at least give Esther and Mordecai permission to write about the situation. In doing so he does more than just permit a letter – he specifies that a decree be issued in his name and sealed with his ring since this is then something that cannot be revoked. Moreover, the letter's content is to be that which pleases Esther and Mordecai. After all, if they have the king's signet ring then what they write has full royal authority, and it is apparently unnecessary to run a draft past the king first. Ahasuerus will have no more direct input into this decree than into Haman's, but the freedom he gives Esther and

---

[15] 1:19.

[16] L. B. Paton (in *A Critical and Exegetical Commentary on the Book of Esther*, p. 270) sees Mordecai's mention as an interpolation, but this stems from his failure to see the events of this chapter as a whole. Mordecai is present all along, though Esther is the dominant figure in the opening verses.

[17] Similarly, M. V. Fox, *Character and Ideology in the Book of Esther* (2nd ed., Grand Rapids: Eerdmans, 2001), p. 94.

[18] 7:8.

Mordecai means they can at least attempt something. There is a wonderful irony in this since the king here commands that a decree be issued in his name so it cannot be revoked, but which is intended to countermand another one of his decrees. There is something intrinsically doubtful about a legal system that establishes irrevocable laws that are capable of being overturned by another decree which simply declares the opposite to apply! Once again, there is more than a hint of satire in dealing with the Persian legal system.

3. Issuing a counter-decree (8:9–14)

With the king's permission it becomes possible for Esther and Mordecai to overcome Haman's decree, and the details of that process are recorded here. Verse 9 is, in fact, the longest single verse in the Bible. The opening of the verse continues the hints of restraint that have so far been apparent – the king's scribes *were summoned* rather than a more direct expression such as, 'Mordecai summoned them'. This is also part of the deliberate patterning of this section on Haman's edict in 3:13. It is apparent that Mordecai is now taking control since it is his command that determines the shape of the decree. The date given in the verse is interesting in that it is seventy days after Haman's decree,[19] though quite how that time has passed is unclear unless there was a significant delay between Haman issuing the decree and the point at which Mordecai brought the matter to Esther's attention. However, *at that time* is often a vague connector and some time may be supposed to have passed in gathering the necessary people before the decree could be issued. The format used for issuing the decree obviously mirrors those of 1:22 and, more precisely, of 3:12, ensuring not only that all levels of Persian government and every province received the decree in the appropriate script and language but also that the Jews received a copy of the decree in their own script and language, even though it was not the language of any particular province. The patterning of Mordecai's decree on Haman's continues in verse 10, where we once again have reference to the courier system, though this time there is an additional note about the horses used. The exact identification of the horses here is uncertain since we have some unusual words that are probably Persian in origin, though the sense is presumably to indicate that these were particularly swift. If so, this highlights the urgency associated with issuing the decree, because even though there are more than eight months remaining,

---

[19] 3:12.

everyone must know that an alternative to Haman's decree exists. Some news simply cannot wait.

Although the process followed by Mordecai is clear enough there are difficulties with the content of his decree. These are both exegetical and ethical, though the resolution of the exegetical issues can largely resolve the ethical ones. As verses 11–12 are commonly interpreted the suggestion would seem to be that the Jews were not only given the right to self-defence, but also to attack and destroy women and children and seize their plunder.[20] Such actions would be entirely inappropriate because it would mean attacking the innocent who are in some way associated with those attacking the Jews but are not themselves involved in it. If this was the intent then we would be right to be repelled by it. The principle of 'an eye for an eye'[21] in the Old Testament is not about gaining unlimited retribution against a foe but rather ensuring that the punishment for a crime matched the damage done but did not exceed it. If Mordecai encouraged additional attacks on innocent women and children then his decree is clearly contrary to this principle. Yet the women and children are not defenceless innocents, but rather are among those attacking the Jews.[22] Lest we think this a strange concept then we need only think back to the attacks in the Holocaust or Bosnia to realise it is entirely plausible. So the offer to the Jews is purely defensive, though a defence where the terms of engagement are shaped through an almost exact series of quotations from 3:12–13 so we understand that this is nothing more than a nullification of Haman's decree. Violence cannot here be avoided, but it can be minimised. The Jews may not initiate anything beyond assembling so they are not isolated. This suggests that Haman's decree prevented them from defending themselves, so Mordecai does not revoke Haman's decree (since this cannot be done) but nullifies it. He must therefore still work within the framework of the Persian state – he does not have the authority to change its structures but must work with them to ensure that the state offers justice to all, empowering the powerless.[23]

One interesting note is that even though permission is given to plunder the enemies, it is explicitly stated at both 9:10 and 9:15 that

[20] E.g. NASB. This interpretation is followed by B. W. Anderson, 'The Book of Esther' in G. W. Buttrick (ed.), *The Interpreter's Bible* vol. 3 (Nashville: Abingdon, 1954), p. 866, among others.

[21] Exod. 21:24; Lev. 24:20; Deut. 19:21.

[22] Robert Gordis, 'Studies in the Esther Narrative', *JBL* 95 (1976), pp. 49–53 makes them part of the Jewish community (cf. NIV), but his view has significant problems. See F. Bush, *Ruth/Esther* (Dallas: Word, 1996), p. 447.

[23] D. Reid, *Esther: An Introduction and Commentary* (Nottingham: IVP, 2008), p. 136.

they refrained from taking any plunder, indicating that they understood the edict as purely defensive. At this stage, only one day is permitted for this defence, a factor made necessary by the fact that Haman's initial decree only granted the one day for the pogrom. Chapter 9:11–15 will provide justification for an extra day in Susa.

Mordecai's approach is an important one for reflection in the post-Christendom world of many Western Christians, where we work from a position of weakness relative to the state, and yet must still operate within the constraints of the state to ensure that which provides benefit for all peoples within the state is achieved. Mordecai does not abandon the essence of his faith but applies this to the good of the state as a whole. This is an issue of emerging importance, particularly as church-based organisations are involved in providing services along with the state, but then find a limit on their ability to share their faith because of the effects of state funding. Mordecai's example provides an important model of how we can work with the state without abandoning the centrality of our faith.

The process reversing Haman's decree is concluded in verses 13–14. The account of the decree's issue is in language that again mirrors Haman's original, but with the distinction that the couriers are now all mounted. That the day was one for vengeance does not mean that the Jews could initiate action against their enemies, since a defensive posture only was permitted. We must understand that although the concept of vengeance in the Old Testament can be one of straightforward revenge, it is not always the case. Certainly, when God's vengeance is described it is often punishment with a view towards restoration.[24] Here, it must be understood in terms of the fact that the enemies were those who would attack the Jews. Vengeance here is thus limited solely to those who attack them.[25] Thus, the mounted couriers hurry to deliver the edict to the provinces which was also published in Susa, driven on by the king's command. Unless this simply means that his authority stood behind Mordecai, it indicates that he had chosen to become involved, accepting his responsibility. If so, we have a decisive change from Haman's earlier decree.

[24] For a helpful discussion of this, see Eric Peels, *Shadow Sides: God in the Old Testament* (Carlisle: Paternoster, 2003), pp. 72–86.
[25] A. Berlin describes it as 'justified retaliation', in *Esther: The Traditional Hebrew Text with the New JPS Translation* (Philadelphia: Jewish Publication Society, 2001), p. 78.

4. The response to the decree (8:15–17)

The contrast between Haman's decree and Mordecai's is made clearer as he enters the city. When Haman was elevated by the king to a high position he needed a decree issued requiring he be paid the appropriate respect. When Mordecai went out from the king in royal robes there is an appropriate response from the people. The royal robes obviously echo the special garments given to him in chapter 6, though the crown is an addition. It is perhaps the typical dress of a Persian noble, similar to what Haman would have worn, but described for the first time here to show the extent of Mordecai's elevation.[26] In response to Mordecai's glorious presence there is shouting and rejoicing in Susa.[27] Mordecai fills Haman's old role, but with a vastly different response. Indeed, the last time Haman had anything to do with the city it was left in a state of confusion (3:15). Mordecai's change of status prepares for special mention of the Jews, at this stage presumably still those in Susa. The use of four terms for joy here undoubtedly parallels the four used for mourning at 4:3. The clothing and situation of the Jews has been completely changed because of a combination of the absolute commitment of God's people and those strange ways in which God is at work. Their rejoicing shows what can be achieved by God's people, even within a potentially hostile state. Moreover, this was not limited to those in Susa, but rather as the decree reached every province the pattern was continued. Mordecai and Esther's work for justice produced celebrations and feasting. Until now, all feasts had been Persian, and we have only had Jewish fasts. But now, it is the Jews who feast and celebrate a 'good day'.[28] Subsequent technical usage in Jewish writings uses this phrase as a term for a religious holiday,[29] for which reason this translation is generally followed. It may well be correct, though we cannot determine the point at which the usage began, but whatever sense is intended it is clear that Mordecai's actions brought much joy.

The final note of the chapter is one of the most unusual. At the end of the verse we are told many *declared themselves Jews*. Taken at face value the statement is remarkable, seeming to suggest mass conversion to an early form of Judaism across the Empire. That this should be recorded in what is seemingly the most secular book in the Old Testament is remarkable. However, the term does not necessarily identify conversion – it could mean that many identified

---

[26] Clines, *Ezra, Nehemiah, Esther*, p. 318. Cf. Gen. 41:42.
[27] Cf. Prov. 11:10.
[28] My translation. The phrase is otherwise found only in 1 Sam. 25:8.
[29] Hence, ESV, 'a holiday'.

themselves with the Jews and their cause, especially since at some points in the book 'Jews' is used as an ethnic description rather than a religious one. Alternatively, it could mean that there was a genuine conversion to Judaism since at other points 'Jewish' has clearly religious overtones, though it does not necessarily require that there was any proselytising.[30] It does perhaps suggest, though, that Jewish faith could be recognised as separate from the ethnic grouping.[31] Such a separation makes it likely that some form of conversion is described, which means the dread could include a sense of religious awe without being limited to it. Perhaps God's otherwise unseen hand is now recognisable to all, continuing the point first seen by Haman's advisers in 6:13, and recognised again by the fear of Mordecai in 9:4.

The chapter is structured to demonstrate the need to continue the task assigned by God beyond the point of resolving personal needs. Mordecai and Esther do not stop simply because Haman is removed. They recognise that they have reached their position for a purpose and that purpose is only fulfilled in the end when they provide a means of escape for the Jews. It is as they carry on their roles, working for justice for all and not just their own people (though that is the pressing need), that the peoples are able to see the presence of God. At the same time it is important to note that although Esther and Mordecai's roles overlap with one another they are not the same. Esther's role here was to bring Mordecai into the government, and he then had the task of offsetting Haman's decree. Thus both contribute to the same goal, but they accept that their part will differ. Paul's directive[32] for Christians to recognise that their different gifts all contribute to the well-being of the church recognises something similar, that working towards the one goal does not mean we all contribute in the same way. Rather, the differing contribution of each needs to be recognised, and each honoured for what it is rather than simply promoting those whose work is more public. This is because what becomes evident here is that the faithful service of God's people has a wider impact than we might anticipate, even in contexts that are not initially positive to it, bringing hope to all.

---

[30] Contra L. B. Paton, *A Critical and Exegetical Commentary on the Book of Esther*, p. 281.

[31] J. G. Baldwin, *Esther: An Introduction and Commentary*, p. 99.

[32] Romans 12:6.

9:1–19
9. Days of deliverance

Haman has been executed and Mordecai has taken his place. Mordecai has now issued a decree[1] that nullifies, but cannot revoke, Haman's.[2] At one level it would therefore seem that all that is needed is to sit and wait for the day to pass. After all, given the dread of the Jews that has fallen on much of the Empire,[3] who would want to attack them? Yet in spite of this, we must still wait to see what actually happens on the thirteenth day of Adar because of the hints of anti-Jewish sentiment within the Empire that we have already noted. Haman's decree could not be revoked, and because Mordecai could only issue a balancing decree the possibility remains that the violence Mordecai's decree sought to minimise might still happen. After all, both the Jews and those who would attack them can claim that the law supports their position. So the tension between the two decrees still needed resolution, for they were contrary to each other. The nature of that resolution is described here, reflecting a gap of more than eight months since the events of chapter 8. But where Mordecai's decree had been the basis for limited feasting by the Jews, the deliverance wrought here will provide the foundation for an enduring practice, a practice hinted at here and developed further and regulated in 9:20 – 10:3, following more work by Mordecai and Esther. In terms of the theology of the book as we have it, the chapter also seeks to answer the question of how providence can be understood. Will God, as unseen but present as ever, vindicate Esther and Mordecai's actions to this point, or will their actions prove fruitless? All the narrative hints to this point suggest a successful outcome, but that outcome needs to be demonstrated in the complete deliverance of the Jews, for only then

[1] 8:11–12.
[2] 3:12–13.
[3] 8:17.

can any significant claims about the nature of God's providential care be made. We have here that demonstration, though again it is one that indicates the important balance between God's involvement and the activity of his people.

1. The day of vengeance (9:1–10)

The chapter opens with a sonorous rendition of the date. It is finally the thirteenth day of the twelfth month, the month of Adar. It is the date set as Haman's lucky day for the destruction of the Jews.[4] But it is not simply a date that was important to Haman, because there is evidence here of widespread anti-Jewish sentiment within the Empire. Such sentiments have not been explicitly mentioned previously, but we noted hints of them in 3:4. In addition, we could agree with Anderson that the narrative presumes that Haman's decree had stirred up such feelings.[5] Thus, whereas so far Haman has been *the enemy of the Jews*[6] the text now speaks of the *enemies* of the Jews. Haman may have been the enemy *par excellence*, the one who inspired such people to action, but he was far from isolated. As always, it is a mistake to imagine that evil thrives simply because there is an individual who promotes it. For evil to flourish there must also be people who are open to its persuasive but destructive charms. This is why it is never sufficient to identify a source of evil within society. Rather, the challenge is to challenge those seduced by it and so to break its charms through the gospel. Even so, its effects will often be greater than we will imagine. So although Esther and Mordecai have worked specifically to address the evil initiated by Haman, they could not have known the extent to which they were also engaged with a far wider problem.

Here we see again a principle demonstrated through the apparent coincidences in 6:1–13. There, Esther used every piece of wisdom available to her, but all that could not have initiated the deliverance she sought unless God was active in some way, however much that activity can only be seen with the perspective of hindsight. Here, Mordecai and Esther have done all they can to nullify Haman's decree, but there was still a large body of people who sought to gain mastery over the Jews, and presumably to gain the plunder from them that was available. Mordecai's decree permitted the Jews to gather and defend themselves, but it could not change the hearts of people who were motivated either by some dislike of the Jews or the

---

[4] 3:7.

[5] B. W. Anderson, 'The Book of Esther' in G. W. Buttrick (ed.), *The Interpreter's Bible* vol. 3 (Nashville: Abingdon, 1954), p. 867.

[6] 3:10; 8:1; and, with variation, 7:6.

simple prospect of easy money to be gained from their destruction. Esther was not able to address the moral problem of Haman's evil with the king, and it turns out that this moral problem is far more deep-seated than we might imagine. The extent of this has so far been hidden from us through the narrator's technique of basically restricting our field of view to that which the characters involved can see, so we might well be surprised by the numbers of those involved in these attacks. Of course, the wider picture of Scripture provides us with a sober assessment of the human heart and its preference for sin,[7] but we do not always expect that inclination to express itself in mass violence. But as those who live this side of the Holocaust, not to mention the genocides in the Balkans or Rwanda, we are no longer as shocked as were former generations who might have thought that human society was leaving such violence behind. But where such violence exists it finds a means to manifest itself, and the arrival of the date stipulated by Haman's decree prepares for its emergence in Persia. But we actually leave Haman behind at this point as the decree is said to be the king's, which of course Haman's use of the royal signet ring made it.[8] Those wishing to attack could thus claim royal support, although the Jews could in turn claim royal support for their defence.

But at the point where these enemies expected to gain mastery something changed. Exactly what that something was is not stated directly, for we simply have a passive verb indicating that the situation was reversed. But the use of passive verbs in Esther is not random, and chapter 2 has already established this as an indirect way of pointing to God. The Jews did not achieve their reversal of fortunes by themselves. Rather, this is as close as the narrator comes to mentioning God directly as the author of the deliverance. Of course, since there is a constant tension within the book of Esther between the achievements of God and those of his people we also read of the Jews gathering for self-defence. Thus, although their enemies had hoped to gain mastery over them, the passive prepares us for the alternative – *the Jews gained mastery over those who hated them.*[9]

The combination of divine intervention with human activity becomes clearer in verses 2–4. The Jews gathered to defend themselves against those who would attack them in their cities and throughout the Empire. It is clear that those who attacked the Jews sought to kill them, so combat to the death is envisaged. Throughout this the Jews are shown acting only in defence. But this is a

---

[7] Gen. 8:21.
[8] 3:12.
[9] 9:1.

powerful defence where no one was able to stand before them. The reason for this success is specifically indicated as the *fear of them*, which seems to be a desacralised reference to God,[10] extending the effect from 8:17. Such dread does not mean any personal recognition of Israel's God, but it does suggest that they knew some divine force was operative for Israel. This element becomes clearer when we remember that the expression that indicates that no one could stand before them is used in the book of Joshua to indicate Yahweh's presence as the one who fights for Israel.[11] The language indicates a division between what the rest of the Empire could perceive and what the Jews should recognise through reflection on their traditions. Indeed, it is by pointing readers to the wider record of Scripture that the book of Esther is able to highlight its own theology. Such a process remains important for Christians today as we consider our experience in light of Scripture and so come to appreciate how God continues to work among us. Such reflection offers insights not available to those outside, who can only see that something is happening, whilst also providing us with a framework for understanding our experience more clearly.

The tension between divine and human assistance is retained in verse 3, though with the reference to the help given to the Jews by the Persian administration system because of the dread of Mordecai that had fallen upon them. The extent of this is emphasised by the solemn listing of the various functionaries within the system, making clear that although there were two royal decrees the administration now saw that Mordecai's people were the ones they should assist. How they helped is unstated, which is perhaps a deliberate narrative gap. But the reason for their *fear of Mordecai* is clearly indicated in verse 4 – his stature in the royal house, and associated renown throughout the Empire, made it politically expedient to accept his suggestions, though we have noted that this position required God's unseen involvement.[12] The *fear* of the Jews and of Mordecai are both expressions of how the inhabitants of the Empire could see something which they could interpret politically, but which the narrator has hinted throughout is more than politics. Yet in doing this, the importance of the wisdom demonstrated by both Esther and Mordecai is never downplayed.

These factors come together in verse 5 to explain the success of the Jews in overcoming their enemies. In making their defence it is obvious that they had great success, though they did not necessarily

---

[10] D. J. A. Clines, *Ezra, Nehemiah, Esther* (Grand Rapids: Eerdmans, 1984), p. 322.
[11] Josh. 21:44; 23:9.
[12] The description of Mordecai here appears to be modelled on that of Moses in Exod. 11:3, anticipating Esth. 10:2–3.

go beyond that which was permitted by the decree. Thus, although they *did as they pleased to those who hated them* it is apparent that this was directed only to those who attacked them, and it was the absence of any intervention by the local members of the government that allowed them such a free hand. Although both Huey and Anderson[13] believe that the Jews must have gone beyond what was decreed, the fact that it was only the enemies who were attacked mitigates against such a suggestion.[14] The enemies of the Jews, as verse 1 makes clear, were those who were prepared to attack them. Indeed, the link with verse 1 is made stronger by describing the enemies as *those who hated them*, repeating the terms from there. Further, repeatedly emphasising that the Jews did not take any plunder suggests that they limited themselves to the terms of Mordecai's decree. If there is also a link throughout the narrative to the events of 1 Samuel 15,[15] then it may be that they were avoiding the mistake Saul had made in his battle with Amalek.[16] Indeed, Saul failed because he took spoil to which he was not entitled, but here the Jews do not take spoil to which they are entitled. Nevertheless, the death of 500[17] people in the citadel of Susa alone suggests either a significant level of anti-Jewish sentiment or at least a large enough group who were prepared to use the first decree as the basis for attempting to seize wealth for themselves at the Jews' expense. Amongst those taken were the sons of Haman, listed in verses 7–9. Although Paton notes that the names are not know elsewhere in Persian documents, and their meaning is uncertain,[18] there is good reason for believing that they are genuine Persian names. Interestingly enough, a scribal tradition stipulates

[13] F. B. Huey, 'Esther', in F. E. Gaebelein (ed.), *The Expositor's Bible Commentary*, vol. 4 (Grand Rapids: Zondervan, 1988), p. 833, Anderson, 'The Book of Esther', p. 867.

[14] A. Berlin notes a similar passage in Herodotus 3.79, describing the massacre of the magi in Persia, in *Esther: The Traditional Hebrew Text with the New JPS Translation* (Philadelphia: Jewish Publication Society, 2001), p. 82. Though similar in many ways to this passage, it notable that the book of Esther is considerably less interested in the blood and guts of violence.

[15] See on 3:1, pp. 60–61.

[16] The link to Amalek seems clear, but the reversal of 1 Sam. 15 is not quite as exact as M. V. Fox suggests (in *Character and Ideology in the Book of Esther* [2nd ed., Grand Rapids: Eerdmans, 2001], p. 115) since it is not Amalekites who are killed here; K. H. Jobes suggests similarly, in his *Esther: The NIV Application Commentary* (Grand Rapids: Zondervan, 1999), p. 198.

[17] Given that the numbers of casualties are all multiples of a hundred, it may be that they represent equivalent military units which were called 'hundreds' and 'thousands', though in practice their size was much smaller. Even if this is the case, the casualties were significant.

[18] L. B. Paton, *A Critical and Exegetical Commentary on the Book of Esther* (Edinburgh: T & T Clark, 1908), p. 71.

that the names are to be printed in two columns, a pattern generally followed in printed editions of the Hebrew Bible today,[19] perhaps to represent the way they died. In spite of their father's death, the sons must have agreed with him and attempted to participate in the pogrom. In any case, the Jews did not take their plunder either, though of course the king had already passed Haman's estate over to Esther. Thus, all that Haman had boasted of has gone to the Jews.[20] The one who sought their destruction has fallen completely before them, just as Zeresh his wife had foretold,[21] while Haman's role in initiating all this is highlighted by once again naming him as *the enemy of the Jews*. The reversal of fortunes for Haman is complete. Proverbs 16:18 insists that pride precedes destruction, and Haman is the classic proof of this.

2. The events in Susa (9:11–15)

Parallel to the more general account from verses 1–10, we also have the more specific detail of verses 11–15, which focuses on the events in the citadel of Susa itself. The opening phrase of verse 11, *That very day*, clearly indicates that the news came to the king promptly regarding the number of those slain, though there is no direct indication that he was also told of the extent of the fighting. Although verse 6 only mentions the non-Jewish casualties, it is improbable that no Jews were killed unless we are intended to see a parallel to the victory over Midian in Numbers 31, where it is explicitly stated that in overcoming their enemies the armies of Israel suffered no losses.[22] But in the absence of any specific allusion we are probably to accept that the author passes over any Jewish casualties so as to highlight the Jews' resounding victory. Not everyone was convinced that the fear of the Jews was sufficient reason not to attack, but God has kept his people even as they also gathered for their own defence.

Apart from this verse, the balance of this section sits oddly within the overall narrative framework. Having reported the 500 killed in the citadel of Susa (as opposed to the rest of the city) to Esther, the king then wonders aloud what will have happened in the rest of the provinces. Ahasuerus is a generally unknowing king, but even he knows that this level of casualties within the citadel indicates that there will be a significant number killed throughout the Empire if the pattern of Susa is repeated. But this does not prepare us for the

[19] Similarly, Josh. 12:9–23.
[20] 5:11.
[21] 6:13.
[22] Num. 31:49.

surprise of his sudden request to Esther asking what she wants. Indeed, without anything being initiated by Esther he largely repeats his earlier questions,[23] though this time he is at least astute enough to realise that offering up to half the kingdom may be a step too far. No reason is given for this decision in verse 12 to ask Esther what she now wanted. That he is rattled by the death of so many (the 500 only being non-Jews) is understandable, but then to ask Esther what else she would like, and to guarantee that she would receive it, lacks any direct motivation. Previously, Esther's actions have at least indicated a desire to be granted something, even if she had to be careful revealing what this was, but here it is entirely the king's initiative. We could understand this as indicating that too many of the king's advisers have fallen, and that this is the final action of a flustered and ineffective monarch.[24] But since Mordecai is still alive this seems unlikely, and it is perhaps more probable that this is how the king demonstrates the fear of the Jews that has affected everyone else. The casualty reports have shown that the Jews are stronger than their attackers, and just as the various provincial leaders have helped them, so also Ahasuerus' offer is his way of seeking the Jews' favour. Thus, the mighty king of 1:1, whose claims to power were so effectively mocked in chapter 1, now understands that his authority is limited in comparison to them. There is a force at work for them that is greater than he has previously encountered, even if he cannot identify it.

However we understand the king's action, Esther's request is even stranger. Since the decrees had only permitted hostility on one day, there was no reason for a second day of vengeance. Even though the king had virtually given Esther *carte blanche* she still phrased her request in the proper language of the court, although there is only one 'if' clause here, whereas previously there has been two. Esther still knows that what she requests must please the king, though given his offer she can be confident of receiving her request. Esther asked for a further day of vengeance for the Jews in Susa to continue to act under the rules of Mordecai's decree, and also that Haman's ten (dead) sons might be impaled, perhaps on the stake he erected for Mordecai. Esther may be addressing a danger not previously revealed, just as the number who would still attack the Jews was unknown. That she is concerned only with Susa, however, suggests she is responding to specific information about the city – she could hardly know about the rest of the Empire, and therefore makes no comment on it. The exposure of the corpses of Haman's

---

[23] 5:6; 7:2.
[24] Cf. Clines, *Ezra, Nehemiah, Esther*, p. 324.

sons would, however, be a powerful signal to those who continued to oppose the Jews, pointing to the king's support for them.[25]

Although the exposure of Haman's sons might warn potential adversaries, it is not impossible that there is an implied criticism of Esther herself at this point, warning of the danger of the abused becoming the abuser. There is a close parallel here with David's exposure of Saul's sons.[26] Even though David did this to overcome Saul's sin, it is notable that Yahweh only responded to the plea for the land after Rizpah's faithfulness saw the bodies properly buried. David could not use faithfulness to Yahweh as a cover for his own acts against Saul's family. If so, we may have an example of an ethical irony in the book,[27] so at the points where Persians become Jews, Jews begin to act like Persians. There is an implicit warning against the seductions of power, even when starting from a position of weakness. In the end, Esther's letter will show her resisting this temptation,[28] but like David it was a temptation that could be seductive. Since the king had already promised Esther her request, it is only natural that it should be granted, though he specifically issues it as law. Accordingly, Haman's ten sons are impaled, and the Jews receive their extra day of vengeance. Who the 300 are who died on the second day is unclear. They are not described as enemies though, since Esther's request requires that the actions of the Jews follow the decree for the previous day, they would still be those who attacked them. In any case, it is again stressed that they laid no hand on the treasure, suggesting that they were still acting in accord with the reserve and faithfulness to the decree that they displayed earlier, so that gaining vengeance on an enemy cannot be the basis for enriching themselves. This second day, however, will also prepare for the two days over which Purim will be celebrated.

3. Events in the provinces (9:16–19)

In parallel with the description of the events in Susa, we are now presented with a description of the events in the provinces. There is a clear parallel between verse 16 and the events of verses 5 to 6, with the additional note that the Jews gained *relief from their enemies*. This relief echoes that which David had been granted by God when he desired to build the temple,[29] aligning

---

[25] Joshua treated the corpses of enemy kings this way – Josh. 10:26.

[26] 2 Sam. 21:1–14.

[27] See Stan Goldman, 'Narrative and Ethical Ironies in Esther', *Journal for Study of the Old Testament* 47 (1990), pp. 15–31.

[28] 9:29–32.

[29] 2 Sam. 7:1, 11.

this deliverance with earlier times in Israel's history, as well as introducing *relief* as a key term in the celebrations that will follow.[30] This is not an isolated moment of deliverance, but stands instead within a pattern of God's activity. Again, the book of Esther points to wider theological themes by pointing readers to interpret these events in light of the wider testimony of Scripture. Laniak also shows that the root from which 'relief' is derived (*nwḥ*) has been carefully deployed through the book.[31] Previously it was initiated by the king (2:18) or used by Haman to show what was not to the king's benefit (3:8). Where the benefit had previously been Persian it has now been reversed through God's unseen providence. Where 800 people were killed in Susa, the figure for the rest of the kingdom was 75,000.[32] That this was also in accordance with the decree only is highlighted by the fact that once again the plunder was not taken. From this derives the explanation of verse 17 that the fourteenth day of Adar had become a day of feasting in the provinces, since the day after the slaughter was a day that they stopped to rest. In contrast, verse 18 points out that those in Susa were gathered for an extra day, so that their day of celebration became the fifteenth of Adar. What is stressed is that the initial celebrations were spontaneous. They required no formal prompting. Hence, the provincial Jews make the fourteenth of Adar the day of feasting, in contrast to the position of the urban Jews who celebrate the feast on the fifteenth, so that urban Jews as a group self-identify with the Jews in Susa.

Although this is not yet called Purim,[33] it is apparent that a plot that was intended to destroy the Jews has instead become a day of feasting and celebration – the ultimate expression of the turning of the tables. The reversal of fortunes that happened at the personal level with Haman's fall has worked itself out for the whole people. As Reid notes, the tradition of sending gifts also allows both for the joy of deliverance to be celebrated, but also for it to be extended within the community.[34] So, a book that began by noting the pretensions to power shown by the Persian king concludes its narrative with the Jews feasting and rejoicing. All has been turned about, and the Jews are delivered. Where the Persians could see only

---

[30] 9:18, 22.

[31] T. S. Laniak, 'Esther', in L. C. Allen and T. S. Laniak, *Ezra, Nehemiah, Esther* (Peabody: Hendrickson, 2003), p. 259. Mordecai uses a different term for 'relief' in 4:14.

[32] The LXX has 15,000.

[33] The title is introduced in 9:26, but we are being prepared for that here.

[34] D. Reid, *Esther: An Introduction and Commentary* (Nottingham: IVP, 2008), p. 146.

a dread power keeping the Jews, they knew there was something more, and so could celebrate.

It may take insights that come only from a deep knowledge of the Scripture to appreciate the ways in which God has been at work, but when that is recognised then celebration and rejoicing is entirely appropriate. What is typical of such celebration in Scripture is that it recognises the importance of giving as a crucial element within it. Celebrating God's goodness to his people is best expressed by sharing that with others, and sharing gifts is one positive way of doing so, though we need to guard against the commercialisation of such processes. Since the giving of gifts here involved portions of food, we might learn again the importance of sharing meals as an act of worship and celebration as opposed to the modern tendency to treat worship only as a formal service. A recent example of this I experienced was when some friends at church celebrated their fiftieth wedding anniversary. They invited many friends and contacts to share with them in attending our normal morning service but then invited them, and the rest of the congregation, to stay and share a lunch that was both a gift of food and a continuation of our worship. Such a gathering was obviously less spontaneous than what is described here (though some in the congregation were effectively invited only during the morning service) but it recognised that sharing with others is a vital element in celebration, and that celebration made sense only in terms of what God had done. It is this that also guides Jewish celebrations here.

The motif that has dominated this section is that of the reversal of Jewish fortunes. The long wait for the dreaded day to come is over, and it was as terrible as many would have feared, though not for the Jews. The passive verb in verse 1 strongly hints that God was involved in changing their circumstances, though the narrative structure also suggests the importance of human involvement. Once again, we are meant to see that they go hand in hand. God's activity works through his people as they are faithful, and so trials turn to joy. However there is also the additional element that distinguishes between the perception of insiders and outsiders. Those who do not know God see only a dread power, but the Jews are able to discern the ways of God through this, and so their feasting and rejoicing already starts to point beyond itself. As Bechtel notes, Psalm 124 might well be the sort of text read at such a celebration: 'If it had not been the LORD who was on our side ...'[35]

---

[35] C. M. Bechtel, *Esther* (Louisville: Westminster John Knox, 2002), p. 78.

9:20 – 10:3
10. Remembering deliverance

A consistent theme throughout Scripture is the importance of pausing to remember those times we have experienced God at work in our lives. The Old Testament emphasises the importance of this, so that Passover and unleavened bread, along with the setting apart of the firstborn, exist to remember how God brought Israel out from Egypt.[1] Similarly, the feast of Tabernacles is a reminder of the period Israel spent in the wilderness and God's goodness to them.[2] But the feasts were not only memories of a distant past. In Deuteronomy the feasts of Weeks and Tabernacles are also celebrations of God's continuing provision through the harvest and that which is made by human craft.[3] Remembering what God has done requires attention to both the great acts of salvation that have shaped the identity of the people of God and his continued sustenance of us. The New Testament similarly recognises the importance of memory. The most obvious example of this is in Jesus' words at the institution of the Lord's Supper, where he indicates that the eating of the bread was in remembrance of him,[4] though in baptism we also remember the work of God in Christ. The Christian calendar has likewise developed so as to help us remember, moving from Advent through Christmas, Lent, Easter, Ascension and Pentecost so we follow that which God has done for us in Christ in our worship. Memory, in particular memory that encourages us to reflect upon how God is active in our lives, is thus an important element in our theological tradition.

The reason for this is that generally it is easier to forget things than remember them, which is why we have these processes to help

[1] Deut. 16:1–8; Exod. 13:2–16.
[2] Lev. 23:33–43.
[3] Deut. 16:8–15.
[4] Luke 22:19; cf. 1 Cor. 11:24–25.

us. The Christian calendar exists as an aid to memory, a reminder of the need to reflect on what God has done for us, though it in turn draws on the pattern already established in the Old Testament and its festivals. But the issue is not simply one of encouraging us to remember, but remembering in a way that helps us focus on what is central to the events we remember. Although the feast of Purim stands outside the central events of deliverance in the Old Testament which are associated with the exodus, it is still an important moment of deliverance that needs to be remembered. That remembrance is both an exuberant celebration and a solemn reflection on what had happened. It is this combination that enables remembrance that truly reflects on what happened and its significance, but which realises that any reflection on God's deliverance ought also to be celebratory. Thus, although many readers find these verses somewhat less engaging than the fast-paced story that has unfolded so far, they offer some important insights for us, explaining why we need to know the story. We know the story so we can remember, and in remembering we reflect on what the story means about God's involvement in our world and our part in that. Hence, although an informal account of Purim's origins has already been provided,[5] this section provides a formalisation of that celebration, perhaps drawing on a range of existing documents which are cited at various points. If so, incorporating these various sources would explain a number of grammatical difficulties and seeming redundancies within this section, though these difficulties may have been exacerbated by scribal attempts to make sense of the text.

1. Mordecai's letter (9:20–28)

The book as a whole is interested in letters, both the foolish such as the decrees of Ahasuerus[6] or Haman,[7] and the wise, such as Mordecai's decree allowing Jews to defend themselves.[8] Thus, these letters stand within a tradition of written communication, though where the earlier communications have been for the whole of the Persian Empire these are specific to the needs of the Jews. The efficient Persian postal service may have been used to initiate a hideous genocide, but it could also be employed both to initiate deliverance and to create a reminder of what has happened that would nourish future generations. In writing these letters, Mordecai

[5] 9:18–19.
[6] 1:19–22.
[7] 3:12–15.
[8] 8:9–12.

131

and Esther both demonstrate that the structures of the state itself are not flawed, only the way that they have been deployed. Both Mordecai and Esther have demonstrated the importance of opposing the abuses of the state, but with these letters they also show that the resources created by the state can be used in ways consistent with the purposes of God. These days, such communication might take place via an email or through some social networking website, but the principle remains the same. Mass communication can be used in ways destructive to the people of God, but a proper understanding of them can also enable a proper appreciation of the work of God.

In Mordecai's case, it was not simply writing a letter. Before that he took the time to write down the events that had happened, because without a clear recollection of what happened it is easy for the events that are celebrated to become blurred. It was this that provided the content of his letters which he was careful to send to all the Jews in the Empire,[9] not just those who were close to Susa. Doing this ensured not only that the days themselves were remembered but also that they were remembered with sufficient content to ensure that the memory was both celebratory and reflective. This record would be more than just the fact of the victory, since this was well known, and the establishment of a perennial celebration would require the background details such as Haman's plan.[10] Levenson also notes that the phrase *near and far* may allude to Isaiah 57:19 so that the events of Purim are seen within the context of a promise of comfort[11] – a further hint that for all the human effort involved, this is still peace brought by God. More than this, there is also an allusion to Jeremiah's promise of a reversal for the exiles, where sorrow was turned to joy and mourning to feasting.[12] That God has been at work is thus made evident through allusion to prophetic hope which is being fulfilled in these events. In particular, allusion to these texts reinforces the point that the Scriptures are themselves the frame through which events are to be interpreted, though it would be fair to say that in the case of the texts noted the fulfilment is in terms of the pattern of how God works rather than being the specific fulfilment of these texts. But again, we see that understanding one part of Scripture

[9] J. G. Baldwin estimates that distances of up to 2,000 miles would have been involved, in *Esther: An Introduction and Commentary* (Leicester: IVP, 1984), p. 108.

[10] So M. V. Fox, *Character and Ideology in the Book of Esther* (2nd ed., Grand Rapids: Eerdmans, 2001), p. 117.

[11] J. D. Levenson, *Esther: A Commentary* (London: SCM Press, 1997), p. 126.

[12] Jer. 31:13. Similarly, T. S. Laniak, 'Esther', in L. C. Allen and T. S. Laniak, *Ezra, Nehemiah, Esther* (Peabody: Hendrickson, 2003), p. 263.

helps understand another, creating a continued dialogue with the whole.

Because of his position, Mordecai could establish the fourteenth and fifteenth of Adar each year as the two days of celebration since these were the days on which deliverance occurred, presumably allowing for the distinction between the urban and rural communities. Rather than requiring celebration on these days it is more likely that Mordecai was regularising the mode of celebration, taking an impromptu event and linking it to the two days over which deliverance had been wrought. But the days were important as the ones when the Jews got relief from their enemies, just as God had provided David with relief from his.[13] The content of Mordecai's letter also alludes to 9:1 in its reference to the reversal of Jewish fortunes, again using the passive verb to hint at God's involvement though without making explicit exactly what it was that God had done. Rather, the record of events is meant to lead to reflection – to a remembrance that considers how God is active within a world where his people are also at work. There is, for the people of God, always a significant theological content to our remembrance, for without this we cannot grasp the richness of what God has done.

Remembrance should also lead to action, though such action is rooted in what is remembered. Thus, the Jews remember that their situation was turned from sadness and mourning into rejoicing and a celebratory day, perhaps a holiday.[14] Remembering good news ought to lead to rejoicing and Mordecai's letter highlights this by making these two days a time of feasting and gladness. There has been a consistent focus on feasting through the book, and where the earlier feasts were Persian, they have progressively become Jewish. Such feasting had been an impromptu response to the initial deliverance, but now it becomes a regulated element, a mechanism to ensure that good news remains good. Good news must be celebrated, and Christians might ponder whether or not we have at times made the good news of Christ seem rather less appealing than it is by losing a sense of celebration. After all, how can anyone know that the deliverance celebrated is good news if it is hidden behind a façade so serious that no one can see how life changing it is?

But the action that remembrance triggers here is not an inward looking celebration. It looks out beyond those who have been delivered to continue to remember others. Thus, food gifts are to be

---

[13] 2 Sam. 7:1, 11. Cf. Esth. 9:16, 18.
[14] See on 8:17, p. 118.

given to others and more general gifts are to be given to the poor. In establishing this, Mordecai links this feast to Israel's earlier feasts, especially Weeks and Tabernacles, both of which stressed the importance of remembering those who lacked independent access to the means of production and so were dependent on others.[15] Of course, this had already happened informally before,[16] so Mordecai effectively taps into a deep awareness of something the Scriptures encourage, but does so to make this an enduring concern of this celebration. Such concern for the poor was also central to Paul's warnings to the church at Corinth when their celebration of the Lord's Supper was actually excluding the poor and creating divisions within the church.[17] Remembering God's deliverance is not only to be celebrated; it is to be celebrated in a way that enables the whole community to rejoice in what God has done, and this can never happen when one part of the community retains all the resources and so excludes others.

Remembrance is not something that happens in isolation. Rather, its meaning is apparent within a community that understands the need to remember and accepts its responsibility to do so. Mordecai had written,[18] but the Jews of the Empire themselves accepted the need to continue what had been begun. Indeed, the initial impetus to celebration had not come from Mordecai but from their own relief at their deliverance. Mordecai's letter has simply regulated the process but its impact is seen in that they accepted the need to continue this process. Their reason for doing so is not so much because Mordecai has written but because they remember what has happened. They remember that Haman was an Agagite, a traditional enemy of God's people,[19] and that as the *enemy of all the Jews*[20] he had plotted to destroy them, casting the *pûr* (the lot[21]) to determine the date *to crush and to destroy them*.[22] But they also remember that the plan was brought to the king's attention[23] and that he permitted the Jews to defend themselves and, on the second

---

[15] Deut. 16:11–15. Cf. Neh. 8:10–12.

[16] 9:19.

[17] 1 Cor. 11:17–22.

[18] Verses 24–25 might summarise the content of Mordecai's letter.

[19] See on 3:1.

[20] Earlier, in 3:10; 7:6; 8:1, he is the 'enemy of the Jews'. By adding 'all' here there may be a sense in which each Jew within the Empire appreciates how Haman was his or her personal adversary, even as the celebration continues to focus on the people as a whole.

[21] See on 3:7, p. 64.

[22] 9:24.

[23] RSV interprets the feminine suffix here as referring to Esther, but as she has not been named it is preferable to understand Haman's plan as the reference, though the text is awkward.

day, to impale Haman's already dead sons as Haman had earlier been. Haman's evil plot thus rebounded onto himself, just as Proverbs suggests it will.[24] This summary of events is brief,[25] and it carefully avoids mention of either Mordecai's or Esther's involvement in bringing this about, perhaps to encourage more reflection on God's part in it, though there is also an element of tact involved if this derives from Mordecai's letter, including a more positive presentation of the king. Either way, remembrance is something that involves the whole community and which has real content on which to reflect.

We are also told that the name of the feast is Purim, apparently the plural form of the Persian word *pûr*. Why the plural is used is not clear, but it may be because of the two days now involved in the celebration, although the festival names of the Old Testament typically take the plural. Whatever the reason, the celebration has a name which is enough to trigger association with the events that have taken place. The combination of Mordecai's letter and the events lead to a decision to continue to remember these days throughout the Empire. More than that, the celebration also includes all who joined them, acknowledging those Persians who aligned themselves with the Jews, and perhaps recognising that Israel as a covenant people had always been open to others joining. Just as a 'mixed multitude'[26] had joined Israel in the exodus, so the events celebrated in Purim follow the pattern of the exodus and include more than just the Jews.[27] There is also a nice pun on the practice of Persian law, since the decision that they would celebrate Purim without fail alludes to 1:19 and 8:8. Persian laws could not be revoked, though they could be nullified, but Purim would never be revoked. Remembrance can continue because the people as a whole acknowledge the need to do so, and the continued celebration of Purim is a reminder that the feast has not been forgotten. Above all, Purim remembers that God has given rest, a gift that should never be forgotten. In the Diaspora today it tends to be celebrated on 14 Adar, though in Israel it is celebrated on 15 Adar, lining up the celebration there with the events in Susa which required the later day of celebration. It is perhaps the most joyous of all the festivals, with one Talmudic text even suggesting that those celebrating could

[24] Prov. 19:21. There may also be an allusion to Gen. 12:3.

[25] We know of no single royal edict that covers all this, but it was initiated by the king's execution of Haman and permission to Mordecai to issue a decree, and it is the compressed nature of the account which makes the reading difficult. Similarly, M. D. Roberts, *Ezra, Nehemiah, Esther* (Dallas: Word, 1993), p. 435.

[26] Exod. 12:38.

[27] Exod. 12:48–49.

reasonably become so drunk they cannot tell the difference between 'Cursed be Haman' and 'Blessed be Mordecai'.[28] Given the extent to which alcohol blurred the decision making of Ahasuerus[29] and Haman[30] it is perhaps not the best advice to follow, but the idea of joyously celebrating the history of God's deliverance ought not to be foreign to Christians, especially as we have the joyous news of Christ.

2. Esther's letter (9:29–32)

Esther too wrote to the Jews scattered throughout the 127 provinces to confirm Mordecai's letter. As with verse 26, the document is described by a somewhat unusual word that perhaps describes an official (and often royal) missive, making clear that this is not simply a note she has prepared. This presumes that the *second* letter about Purim is Esther's own since we only have one letter from Mordecai mentioned so far. Mordecai is associated with this document too, though the feminine verb indicates that this is still Esther's letter.[31] This is somewhat complicated by verse 30 which has a masculine verb, leading NIV to translate, 'And Mordecai sent...', though Mordecai is not actually named there. More probably, we should read the verb there impersonally, and follow ESV's 'Letters were sent...'[32] Although Mordecai clearly cooperates with Esther, this is Esther's contribution to remembrance. There is also great weight to the way Esther herself is introduced here with both her Persian title (Queen) and Jewish ancestry mentioned, indicating again her place as the one who holds Jewish and Persian interests together. Esther's authority is also stressed as she too obliges the Jewish communities to observe the days of Purim.

These letters are an example of the biblical principle of establishing matters on the testimony of two or three witnesses.[33] Although this law was initially focused on the testimony needed to convict someone of a capital charge, Paul adapts this principle to consider

---

[28] *Megillah* 7a.

[29] 1:10–12.

[30] 5:9–14.

[31] Numerous scholars suggest that reference to Mordecai here is a scribal error – e.g. F. Bush, *Ruth/Esther* (Dallas: Word, 1996), pp. 468–471. Omission of Mordecai here makes for a much easier text, but we still need to explain how such an odd text was created, and it would be easier to explain Mordecai's omission than his inclusion. Hence, the reference to Mordecai is here treated as an aside that does not contribute to the narrative flow.

[32] Admittedly, such a construction more normally would employ a plural verb, but the singular is not impossible.

[33] Num. 35:30.

the wider context of sin within the community.[34] But there is no reason why this principle should only apply when judging sin since we also need to confirm claims for the work of God on a similar basis. That is what Esther offers us here with a message that was one of peace and truth.

When we pause to celebrate what God has done among us, then peace and truth ought to characterise our own speech. It is easy to slip over into unnecessary triumphalism which can be offensive to others, but Esther's letter avoids this. It recognises that the Jews remained a minority community, so although the truth about what God has done had to be communicated, it had to be done in a sensitive manner. More than that, it also alludes to Zechariah 8:19, a prophetic promise of fasting being changed to feasting, and which also leads to many seeking to join the Jews. Purim is thus seen as a sign of that eschatological moment when many would join the people of God. This process already may have begun in 8:17, but if so it is only a small foretaste of what the New Testament announces has arrived in the resurrection of Jesus and the gift of the Spirit at Pentecost.[35] Nevertheless, by putting this in the context of a celebration of what God had done, Esther reminds us that our celebrations are simultaneously a thanksgiving for what God has done and an anticipation of what he will do. That is why Paul can affirm that when we celebrate the Lord's Supper we 'proclaim the Lord's death until he comes'.[36]

There is a further dimension that Esther's letter adds even as it confirms what had already been established through Esther and Mordecai in recognising that Purim was to be celebrated. Mordecai's letter had emphasised the celebratory aspect of the festival, speaking of feasting, gladness and sharing gifts.[37] Esther's letter not only confirms this and its importance for subsequent generations of Jews,[38] it also ensures that these were to be days with an emphasis on fasting and lamentation. This, of course, had marked the behaviour of the Jews when word of Haman's initial decree reached them,[39] and acknowledgement of it is something Esther requires of them in their commemoration of Purim, which is why some Jews have fasted on Adar 13. There is a sense in which we can only appreciate the wondrous joy of deliverance if we also remember the pain and terror that preceded it, so Esther's emphasis

---

[34] 2 Cor. 13:1.
[35] Acts 2:1–41.
[36] 1 Cor.11:26.
[37] 9:22.
[38] 9:27.
[39] 4:3.

becomes a mechanism for ensuring that this is not lost amid the general merrymaking. Pain and praise invariably belong together, for only when we remember the pain does our thanksgiving come to have real content, and it is this that is protected here. After all, even a people who celebrate deliverance at one point know there will be other times of pain ahead. Perhaps this is why the book of Esther was so important to many who lived through the Holocaust.[40] By way of a small scale analogy, it is worth noting that within the Christian tradition we have often encouraged times of testimony which focus on thanksgiving for God's deliverance of someone from a specific situation, though perhaps we are not as strong at inviting congregants to share their times of pain as well, so that our thanksgiving can more truly join with theirs. The benefit of including pain with praise is that we do not thereby exclude those who are passing through periods of difficulty, and thus also point them to our hope in God. Putting this in writing enabled Esther to authorise this element in the celebration of Purim, with her *command* thus equal in authority to Ahasuerus,[41] making her the only woman in Scripture to write and establish such an event.[42]

3. Mordecai's greatness (10:1–3)

After all the events described in the book, life finally returns to normal. Normal life here includes the payment of tax, though in this case the tax imposed by Ahasuerus might have been either a period of forced labour or a cash sum since the word used could mean either. But where the Jews had been particularly singled out in earlier events, the king now taxes the whole of the kingdom, reaching out to its distant islands. Sudden mention of taxation is perhaps something of a surprise at this point, but the Empire has been through an expensive period with the near destruction of one of its peoples. Ahasuerus has also failed to receive the bribe promised by Haman. It is an unpleasant reality since taxation is never popular, but it means routine government has returned, and that has been lacking for some time. Deliverance has been achieved and everyone, Jew and Persian, can return to normal life.

Ahasuerus remains the great king and his achievements could apparently be accessed in the Chronicles of Persia and Media, the book he had earlier had read to him while trying to sleep, from

---

[40] See K. H. Jobes, *Esther: The NIV Application Commentary* (Grand Rapids: Zondervan, 1999), p. 220.

[41] The word *ma'ămār* ('command') occurs in the Old Testament only here, in 1:15 (where it refers to Ahasuerus) and in 2:22 (referring to Mordecai).

[42] Jobes, *Esther*, p. 224.

which he discovered that Mordecai remained unrewarded for providing the information that saved his life.[43] But that oversight has now been rectified, and special mention is made of the high honour to which the king had advanced Mordecai. Esther is not mentioned here because hers was not seen as a functional role within government, whereas Mordecai's was. Honour had been the centre of the discussion between Ahasuerus and Haman, though only Ahasuerus had known it was about honour for Mordecai, whereas Haman fondly imagined that the honour would be his.[44] Where the honour Haman had proposed had been a fantasy of being advanced to virtual equality with the king, rather than more typical rewards of power and wealth, that situation now has been corrected. Mordecai now has been honoured properly. More than that, he (like Joseph before him[45]) is second only to the king and great among the Jews. In an Empire that was prepared to destroy all Jews, Mordecai's status is itself a pointer to the protection God gave his people. But Mordecai's greatness was also seen in his popularity among his brothers – here a reference to his fellow Jews – seeking that which was good for them and promoting peace.

Mordecai is thus presented as a model for Jews within the Empire; someone who sees that a deliverance once received is not the end of the matter, but that there is an ongoing need to develop that which promotes the well-being of the people of God without neglecting his civil responsibilities to the king. Paul understood this when he expressed his concern that Christians should work for the good of all, especially those of the household of faith.[46] For Mordecai this could now be achieved within the constraints of the Empire, though it is an Empire that is always approached with a degree of caution. Nevertheless, he shows that with proper awareness it is possible to remain committed to your people and still achieve that which is necessary for the good of the Empire as a whole. This is a model that remembers, just as Purim requires memory, but which also looks forward to the contribution that can still be made. In the post-Christendom world in which we live, this remains an important model for believers who understand and remember the good news of our deliverance in Christ and who also recognise that God continues to involve himself in this world, even if that often happens through the commitment of his people. As the book of Esther recognises, how we balance this out remains a challenge that requires wisdom, care and also God's providential

[43] 6:1–3.
[44] 6:6–9.
[45] Gen. 41:40.
[46] Gal. 6:10.

care beyond that, since we can do nothing without him. The challenge remains, but it is one that the book encourages us to consider, drawing encouragement from the memory of what God has done, sharing in celebration with his people, and continuing to work for his peace. This, after all, is what the gospel demands of us.

The Bible Speaks Today: Old Testament series

The Message of Genesis 1 – 11
The dawn of creation
David Atkinson

The Message of Genesis 12 – 50
From Abraham to Joseph
Joyce G. Baldwin

The Message of Exodus
The days of our pilgrimage
Alec Motyer

The Message of Leviticus
Free to be holy
Derek Tidball

The Message of Numbers
Journey to the promised land
Raymond Brown

The Message of Deuteronomy
Not by bread alone
Raymond Brown

The Message of Judges
Grace abounding
Michael Wilcock

The Message of Ruth
The wings of refuge
David Atkinson

The Message of Samuel
*Personalities, potential, politics
and power*
Mary Evans

The Message of Chronicles
One church, one faith, one Lord
Michael Wilcock

The Message of Nehemiah
God's servant in a time of change
Raymond Brown

The Message of Esther
God present but unseen
David G. Firth

The Message of Job
Suffering and grace
David Atkinson

**The Message of Psalms
1 – 72**
Songs for the people of God
Michael Wilcock

**The Message of Psalms
73 – 150**
Songs for the people of God
Michael Wilcock

The Message of Proverbs
Wisdom for life
David Atkinson

The Message of Ecclesiastes
*A time to mourn, and a time to
dance*
Derek Kidner

**The Message of the Song of
Songs**
The lyrics of love
Tom Gledhill

The Message of Isaiah
On eagles' wings
Barry Webb

The Message of Jeremiah
Against wind and tide
Derek Kidner

The Message of Ezekiel
A new heart and a new spirit
Christopher J. H. Wright

The Bible Speaks Today: New Testament series

The Message of the Sermon on the Mount (Matthew 5 – 7)
Christian counter-culture
John Stott

The Message of Matthew
The kingdom of heaven
Michael Green

The Message of Mark
The mystery of faith
Donald English

The Message of Luke
The Saviour of the world
Michael Wilcock

The Message of John
Here is your King
Bruce Milne

The Message of Acts
To the ends of the earth
John Stott

The Message of Romans
God's good news for the world
John Stott

The Message of 1 Corinthians
Life in the local church
David Prior

The Message of 2 Corinthians
Power in weakness
Paul Barnett

The Message of Galatians
Only one way
John Stott

The Message of Ephesians
God's new society
John Stott

The Message of Philippians
Jesus our Joy
Alec Motyer

The Message of Colossians and Philemon
Fullness and freedom
Dick Lucas

The Message of Thessalonians
Preparing for the coming King
John Stott

The Message of 1 Timothy and Titus
The life of the local church
John Stott

The Message of 2 Timothy
Guard the gospel
John Stott

The Message of Hebrews
Christ above all
Raymond Brown

The Message of James
The tests of faith
Alec Motyer

The Message of 1 Peter
The way of the cross
Edmund Clowney

The Message of 2 Peter and Jude
The promise of his coming
Dick Lucas and Christopher Green

The Message of John's Letters
Living in the love of God
David Jackman

The Message of Revelation
I saw heaven opened
Michael Wilcock

The Bible Speaks Today: Bible Themes series

The Message of the Living God
His glory, his people, his world
Peter Lewis

The Message of the Resurrection
Christ is risen!
Paul Beasley-Murray

The Message of the Cross
Wisdom unsearchable, love indestructible
Derek Tidball

The Message of Salvation
By God's grace, for God's glory
Philip Graham Ryken

The Message of Creation
Encountering the Lord of the universe
David Wilkinson

The Message of Heaven and Hell
Grace and destiny
Bruce Milne

The Message of Mission
The glory of Christ in all time and space
Howard Peskett and Vinoth Ramachandra

The Message of Prayer
Approaching the throne of grace
Tim Chester

The Message of the Trinity
Life in God
Brian Edgar

The Message of Evil and Suffering
Light into darkness
Peter Hicks

The Message of the Holy Spirit
The Spirit of encounter
Keith Warrington

The Message of Holiness
Restoring God's masterpiece
Derek Tidball